Ursula's Italian Cakes and Desserts

Ursula's Italian Cakes and Desserts

Ursula Ferrigno

edited by Susanna Tee

metro

First published in Great Britain in 1997
by Metro Books (an imprint of Metro Publishing Limited),
19 Gerrard Street, London W1V 7LA

British Library Cataloguing in Publication Data. A CIP record of this
book is available on request from the British Library.

ISBN 1 900512 27 0

10 9 8 7 6 5 4 3 2 1

Typeset by SX Composing DTP, Rayleigh, Essex.
Illustrations by Madeleine Hardie
Photographs by Jean Cazals
Food Stylist Maria Huxley

Printed in Finland by WSOY

Ursula Ferrigno was born in Southern Italy to an Italian father and English mother and grew up in an environment where family life was centred around the kitchen table. The quality and taste of food was of paramount importance and her enthusiasm for cooking continued after her move to England, where she went on to become a professional chef. Ursula set up the first vegetarian restaurant in north west England and its success prompted Ursula to try her hand at writing.

Her first book, *The 90's Vegetarian*, published in 1994, contains recipes inspired by the Mediterranean and, a year later, Ursula wrote her second book, *Pizza, Pasta and Polenta*. Her next book, *Real Fast Vegetarian Food* stayed in *The Sunday Times* Bestseller list for over three months. She is already planning a fifth book.

As well as her work as a writer, Ursula is a passionate cookery teacher. She was the principal tutor for The Vegetarian Society, head teacher at The Cordon Vert Cookery School and now runs highly successful courses at the Books for Cooks Cookery School as well as in Italy. She is a frequent demonstrator at the BBC Good Food Shows and has become a valued food consultant for a number of major companies and has recently been appointed Cookery Editor of supermarket chain Tesco's magazine. Ursula is also a regular television and radio broadcaster.

Dedication

To all my family who give me so much support and my late Grandmother for her stories, recipes and love of good food upon which I have built my career.

Acknowledgements

I am extremely grateful to:

HEIDI LACELLES of the famous Books for Cooks shop for her kindness and support.

MICHÈLLE BARLOW for her help and advice.

ROSIE and ERIC, BRIDGET CHAPMAN, HEATHER OWEN, SUSANNE MCDADD, CHERYL LANYON and MY MAN IN ROME.

GALBANI for their constant flow of delicious cheese, which I strongly recommend and use in my recipes.

BODUM for their ever-stylish and practical equipment that enhances my work.

MAGIMIX for my machinery, which I cherish, particularly my Gelato 2000.

Last, but by no means least, SUSANNA TEE, who has edited this book diligently and determinedly.

CONTENTS

Introduction

Cakes and pastries are synonymous with Italy. Relaxing mornings are spent sitting in the piazzas, being lured into a noisy bar for a dark espresso or a bubbly, foamy cappuccino, accompanied by a cream cake or a freshly-made, almond-filled, pastry. Later, at lunch time, an apéritif is enjoyed along with a sweet biscuit or macaroon.

Few travellers return from Italy without lasting memories of the delicious ice cream. I have included a complete chapter of recipes for ice creams and water ices, which I hope will inspire you to make your own rather than buying them ready-made. The traveller will also find wonderful speciality cakes and desserts in the many towns and villages throughout Italy. Many of the traditional recipes have been developed to use the abundance of fruit and other produce found in the different regions and, with so many to choose from, I have included a selection of my favourites.

It is a wonderful Italian tradition to give gifts of food at all times, so I am delighted to share with you in the chapter on Gifts of Food, some of the very best sweet treats, liqueurs and bottled fruits I know of, which always make welcome offerings wherever you go.

The recipes in **Italian Cakes and Desserts** have been collected from family and friends and I do hope that you will enjoy my collection.

Ursula Ferrigno

Cookery Notes

For all the recipes, quantities are given in metric and imperial. Follow one set of measurements but not a mixture as they are not interchangeable. You may notice that a certain measurement is not translated in exactly the same way in every recipe. This is because the conversions can never be exact and, in some cases, rounding the conversion up or down can make a better balance of ingredients for a particular recipe.

• Sets of measuring spoons are available in both metric and imperial sizes and have been used in all the recipes to give accurate measurements of small quantities.

• Spoon measures are level.
• Medium eggs are used in the recipes unless otherwise stated.
• Granulated sugar, white or brown, is used unless otherwise stated.

Italian Names
Most of the recipes in this book have been given an English name, to translate the original Italian and give you some idea of what the dish is like. The Italian is always given as well, so you can recognise a dish if you've had it before, or you speak Italian. Some dishes are so well-known by their Italian name that they are not translated, as they will be familiar to almost everyone.

The Store Cupboard

It's always worth having some essentials for making delicious cakes and desserts in your store cupboard, so you know you will have the basics you will need if you want to make something sweet at short notice. It will prevent unnecessary journeys to the shops which are so annoying, especially if you are in the middle of cooking.

Here is a list of some of the essentials I think it is worth keeping in your store cupboard.

Grains
'OO' grade Italian flour
Plain flour
Self raising flour
Polenta

Oils
Olive oil is really the only oil to use for cooking these sweet things.

Nuts
Almonds – whole, blanched, flaked and ground – I use lots of almonds.
Whole hazelnuts
Pistachios – unsalted, of course
Pine kernels

Spices and flavourings
Ground cinnamon and cinnamon sticks to grind freshly yourself.
Fennel seeds
Cloves
Nutmeg
Vanilla pod and vanilla extract
Almond extract
Orange flower water

Dried fruits
Dried fruits have wonderful, concentrated flavours that work well in desserts. If possible, choose those that are not preserved with sulphur dioxide as they have more flavour and nutritional value.
Figs
Apricots
Raisins

Candied orange and lemon zest (you can make this yourself from the recipe on page 204, then store it).

Sugar
Granulated sugar – for many, general purposes
Icing sugar makes a wonderful decoration, sifted over cakes and desserts.
Caster sugar
Soft brown sugar

Miscellaneous
Strong espresso coffee beans
Chocolate with 70 per cent cocoa solids and chocolate with 50 per cent cocoa solids. Chocolate will deteriorate eventually, but can be kept for several weeks in a cool place.
Amaretto biscuits – these are dry and hard and will keep for several months in a closed packet or tin.
Cocoa powder for sifting over cakes and desserts
Fragrant honey
Salt
Baking powder
Dried yeast

Alcoholic drinks
These are obviously expensive to buy and you may not want to stock them all. But they will last a long time if you only use them for cooking, so you could build up your collection slowly.
Marsala
Light and dark rum
Brandy
Amaretto liqueur
Vodka

The Best Italian Desserts

Italy is rich in desserts so this chapter was easy to write – the only trouble being that I had so many recipes to choose from. I hope you will enjoy trying them all. You may have already tasted them in restaurants, but I feel sure they will be even better in your own home. You will find some true Italian classics, such as Zabaglione and Panna Cotta, as well as some more unusual things, such as Apostles' Fingers and Coffee Ricotta.

ZABAGLIONE

This is a most fabulous Sicilian pudding. The delicious foam is so rich it is best accompanied by fresh fruit. It was once prescribed by Italian doctors as a pick-me-up. It really does produce a good, warm feeling.

SERVES 2

2 egg yolks
30ml (2 tablespoons) caster sugar

30ml (2 tablespoons) Marsala

- Put the egg yolks in a large, heatproof bowl or in the top pan of a double boiler and whisk together. When the mixture starts to thicken, place the bowl over a saucepan of gently simmering water.

- Add the Marsala and whisk continuously until the mixture becomes thick, hot and foamy.

- Spoon into serving dishes and serve at once.

PANNA COTTA

This dessert is eaten mainly in the north of Italy where dairy produce is used to a great extent. It is very rich, so servings are small and I like to serve it with a purée of apricots that have been soaked in brandy and lemon juice.

SERVES 4

300ml (½ pint) double cream
30ml (2 tablespoons) sugar or
   more to taste
8 drops of vanilla extract

10ml (2 teaspoons) agar agar or
   15ml (1 tablespoon) powdered
   gelatine

- Put the cream, sugar and vanilla extract in a saucepan and simmer for 2-3 minutes.

- Dissolve the agar agar or gelatine in approximately 30ml (2 tablespoons) warm water. Beat well into the cream.

- Pour into a small serving bowl or 4 individual bowls or ramekin dishes. Chill in the fridge for 2-3 hours before serving.

CHESTNUT AND CHOCOLATE PUDDINGS

Budinos di Castagne e Cioccolato

The chestnut grows extensively throughout Italy and has been called the ultimate in organic food as it grows solely with the help of rainwater and sunlight. In Italy, we often cook chestnuts with bay leaves for the mild flavour they impart.

SERVES 8

700g (1½lb) fresh chestnuts or 435g can unsweetened chestnut purée
3 bay leaves
175g (6oz) dark chocolate with 70 per cent cocoa solids
175g (6oz) caster sugar
175g (6oz) unsalted butter
2.5ml (½ teaspoon) vanilla extract
45ml (2fl oz) dark rum
220ml (7fl oz) double cream
whipped cream and cocoa powder, to serve (optional)

- If using fresh chestnuts, pierce each one and put in a saucepan with the bay leaves and cover with water. Bring to the boil, then simmer for 25 minutes until tender. Drain and, as soon as they are cool enough to handle, remove the shells and skin.

- Put in a food processor and blend to form a purée.

- Put the chocolate, sugar, butter, vanilla and rum in a saucepan. Heat gently until the sugar has dissolved, then add the fresh or canned chestnut purée.

- Remove from the heat and mix together until the ingredients are well blended. Pour into a large bowl and leave to cool.

- Whip the cream until it just holds its shape, then fold into the cooled mixture.

- Spoon the mixture into 8 ramekin dishes and chill in the fridge for 2-3 hours until firm and set.

- If liked, serve topped with a little cream and a dusting of sifted cocoa powder.

STUFFED PEACHES

Pesche Ripiene

There are not many old Italian desserts but this is one of the classics. It is Sergio Torelli's recipe; he's the head chef at Savini's, Milan's famous restaurant near the Duomo.

SERVES 6

25g (1oz) unsalted butter plus extra, for greasing
6 yellow peaches
100g (4oz) whole blanched almonds
12 Amaretti biscuits (almond macaroons)
50g (2oz) sugar

1 egg yolk
30ml (2 tablespoons) Marsala, Maraschino or Amaretto (almond liqueur)
grated zest of ½ lemon
50ml (2fl oz) white wine
icing sugar, to serve

- Pre-heat the oven to 180°C, 350°F, Gas Mark 4. Butter a shallow, ovenproof dish.

- Cut the peaches in half and remove the stones. Place the halves in the prepared dish, cut side up.

- Put the almonds and Amaretti biscuits in a food processor and coarsely grind. Mix in 50g (2oz) of caster sugar, the egg yolk, Marsala and lemon zest.

- Use the mixture to stuff the peach halves, piling it up slightly. Sprinkle over the wine. Place a shaving of butter on top of each peach half.

- Bake in the oven for about 20 minutes until the peaches are soft but still holding their shape.

- Serve dusted with sifted icing sugar.

CHOCOLATE MOUSSE

Mousse di Cioccolato

This mousse has an almost chocolate truffle-type consistency and is very, very rich. The recipe was given to me by my friend Claudio who lives in Perugia.

SERVES 6-8

175g (6oz) dark chocolate with 70 per cent cocoa solids
450ml (¾ pint) whipping cream

2 free range eggs, separated
50g (2oz) chopped, toasted hazelnuts

- Break the chocolate into pieces and put in a heatproof bowl over a saucepan of barely simmering water. As soon as the chocolate has melted, remove the bowl from the heat and leave until it has cooled but is still liquid.

- Whip the cream until it just holds its shape. Fold in the beaten egg yolks.

- Whisk the egg whites until stiff but not dry. Fold the cream into the chocolate then the hazelnuts. Lastly, fold in the egg whites.

- Spoon into a serving dish and chill in the fridge for 4 hours before serving.

COCONUT AND HAZELNUT PUDDING

Budino di Semola

Literally translated, Budino di Semola *means Semolina Pudding, but do not be put off by thoughts of school meals. With the addition of coconut and hazelnuts, this is surprisingly delicious and is made throughout Sicily.*

MAKES 20 SLICES

225g (8oz) semolina
225g (8oz) desiccated coconut
225g (8oz) caster sugar
grated zest and juice of 1 lemon
10ml (2 teaspoons) vanilla extract
100g (4oz) unsalted butter
568ml (1 pint) milk
15ml (1 tablespoon) plain white or Italian type '00' flour
5ml (1 teaspoon) cinnamon
100g (4oz) hazelnuts or almonds
icing sugar, to serve
mascarpone cheese or thick double cream, to serve

- Pre-heat the oven to 180°C, 350°F, Gas Mark 4.

- Put all the ingredients, except the nuts, in a saucepan and mix together. Slowly bring to the boil, stirring all the time. Remove from the heat and leave to cool. The mixture at this stage should be thick, like porridge.

- Press the mixture into a Swiss roll tin. (It should be only 1cm (½ inch) thick.) Roughly chop the hazelnuts or almonds and sprinkle over the top to decorate.

- Bake in the oven for 20 minutes. Lightly dust with sifted icing sugar, cut into squares and serve hot or cold. Accompany with mascarpone cheese or cream.

HONEY BALLS

Cicerchiata

We particularly eat these at Christmas time but I would not limit their enjoyment to once a year! Children just love them.

SERVES 4

250g (8oz) plain white or Italian type '00' flour
25g (1oz) unsalted butter
125g (5oz) caster sugar
2 free range eggs, lightly beaten

about 15ml (1 tablespoon) dry white wine
olive oil, for deep fat frying
100g (4oz) fragrant honey

- Using a fork, mix together the flour, butter, 25g (1oz) of the sugar, the eggs and the wine to make a soft dough. Add 5ml (1 teaspoon) extra wine, if needed.

- On a lightly floured surface, lightly knead the dough then pinch off pieces about the size of a chestnut or small apricot and roll into balls. This will make about 20 small balls.

- Heat the olive oil then fry the dough balls in the hot oil until they are golden. Drain on kitchen paper.

- In a small saucepan, slowly heat the remaining sugar and honey to form a caramel, taking care not to let the mixture boil.

- On a serving dish, pile the balls into a pyramid, pour over the caramel sauce and turn the balls to coat. Serve immediately, with a little extra sauce poured over.

ROMAN CHEESECAKE

Torta Romana

I first enjoyed this recipe in Rome when my colleagues and I stumbled across an excellent café. The cheesecake is light, yet rich and creamy, and so easy to make.

SERVES 8

butter, for greasing
30ml (2 tablespoons) fresh breadcrumbs
50g (2oz) dried or 100g (4oz) fresh apricots
30ml (2 tablespoons) seedless raisins
50ml (2fl oz) Marsala or Amaretto (almond liqueur)
700g (1½lb) ricotta cheese
100g (4oz) honey
2 free range eggs, separated
grated zest of 1 unwaxed lemon

- Pre-heat the oven to 180°C, 350°F, Gas Mark 4. Generously butter the base and sides of a 20cm (8 inch) springform or loose-bottomed cake tin. Dust with the breadcrumbs, covering the base and sides as evenly as possible.

- Finely chop the dried or fresh apricots. Soak the dried apricots and raisins in the liqueur for 30 minutes.

- Sieve the ricotta cheese into a large bowl and beat in the honey and egg yolks. Stir in the soaked fruit and the liqueur, fresh apricots, if using, and the lemon zest.

- Whisk the egg whites until stiff but not dry, then fold into the cheese mixture.

- Pour into the prepared tin and bake in the oven for 50 minutes-1 hour until a skewer, inserted in the centre, comes out clean. Cool in the tin for 2-3 minutes, then remove from the tin and transfer to a wire cake rack, still on its base, and leave to cool completely.

ORANGE SOUFFLÉ

Sformato di Arancia

A sformato *is not unlike a soufflé but has the texture of a pudding. It is a very old dish that was originally served at banquets in the seventeenth century and today is mainly cooked in Italian homes rather than in restaurants.*

SERVES 10

3 medium juicy oranges
5ml (1 teaspoon) coarse-grained salt
225g (8oz) blanched almonds
50g (2oz) broken walnuts
6 extra large free range eggs, separated
225g (8oz) caster sugar plus 30ml (2 tablespoons)
5ml (1 teaspoon) orange flower

water
100g (4oz) granulated sugar
10ml (2 teaspoons) lemon juice
100g (4oz) toasted blanched almonds
225ml (8oz) double cream
5ml (1 teaspoon) icing sugar
50ml (2fl oz) light rum
shredded zest of 1 orange, to decorate

- Put the whole oranges in a large bowl. Add 1 litre (2 pints) of cold water and the salt and leave to soak for 1 hour.

- Drain and wash the oranges, then put them in a small saucepan with 1 litre (2 pints) of cold water. (The oranges should be completely covered by the water.) Put the pan over a medium heat. Bring to the boil, cover and simmer for 45 minutes. Drain and leave the oranges to cool.

- When cool, cut the oranges in half and remove the pips. Put the oranges in a food processor and blend until smooth. Pour into a bowl.

- Finely chop the blanched almonds and walnuts and add to the oranges.

- Pre-heat the oven to 200°C, 400°F, Gas Mark 6. Butter and lightly flour a 22cm (8½ inch) soufflé dish.

- Put the egg yolks and 225g (8oz) caster sugar in a bowl and whisk until thick and creamy. Add the orange flower water and mix well together. Pour the mixture into the bowl with the oranges and nuts and mix very well.

- Whisk the egg whites until stiff but not dry, then fold into the mixture.

- Turn the mixture into the prepared dish and bake in the oven for I hour until firm to the touch and a skewer, inserted in the centre, comes out clean. Remove from the oven and leave to stand for 1 hour.

- To make the syrup, put 225ml (8fl oz) water and the granulated sugar in a small saucepan. Put the pan over a low heat until the sugar has dissolved, then bring to the boil, add the lemon juice and simmer for 10 minutes until a thick syrup is formed.

- Meanwhile, line a cake stand with baking parchment and turn the soufflé out onto it.

- Roughly chop the toasted almonds.

- Whisk the cream until it just holds its shape, then add the 30ml (2 tablespoons) caster sugar and the icing sugar.

- When the syrup is ready, brush on the sides of the soufflé to moisten, then cover the sides with the chopped almonds. Leave to stand for 5 minutes so that the almonds become attached to the soufflé.

- Transfer the soufflé to a serving plate and pour over the rum. Spoon the whipped cream on top to decorate and sprinkle over the orange shreds.

CREAM AND MARSALA TRIFLE

Zuppa Inglese
(See colour photograph)

There are many variations of this very popular dessert, which is served in many restaurants throughout Italy. Loosely translated it means English soup, but in fact it is a rich cream trifle.

SERVES 8

For the cake
butter, for greasing
3 free range eggs
100g (4oz) caster sugar
100g (4oz) plain white or Italian
   type '00' flour
2.5ml (½ teaspoon) baking powder
45ml (3 tablespoons) Marsala
For the crème Anglaise
450ml (¾ pint) milk

4 large egg yolks
75g (3oz) caster sugar
2.5ml (½ teaspoon) salt
5ml (1 teaspoon) vanilla extract
grated zest of ½ an unwaxed lemon
For the topping
300ml (½ pint) double cream
a few toasted flaked almonds, to
   decorate

- Pre-heat the oven to 180°C, 350°F, Gas Mark 4. Brush a 20cm (8 inch) springform cake tin thoroughly with a little melted butter.

- Beat together the eggs and sugar for 10-15 minutes until thick and creamy.

- Sift the flour and baking powder together then, using a metal spoon, fold into the egg mixture.

- Put the mixture into the prepared tin and bake in the oven for 20 minutes until the cake is golden and has shrunk away from the sides of the tin. Leave to cool in the tin.

- When cool, remove from the tin and place the cake in a large, heatproof serving bowl or individual serving dishes. Pour over the Marsala, break up the cake a little and set aside.

- Meanwhile, prepare the crème Anglaise. In a saucepan, bring the milk to just below boiling point and keep it hot. In a bowl, whisk together the egg yolks, sugar and salt until pale and fluffy. Pour in the hot milk, stirring with a wooden spoon. Return the mixture to a clean pan and heat gently, stirring all the time, until the mixture thickens and coats the back of a wooden spoon. Stir in the vanilla extract and lemon zest and pour over the cake. Leave until cold.

- When cold, whip the cream until it holds its shape, then use to cover the crème Anglaise. Scatter over the almonds to decorate.

STUFFED PEARS WITH A CHOCOLATE COATING

Pere Cotte Ricoperte di Cioccolata

I can't think of a better combination than pears and chocolate. Do use ripe pears. I like Williams pears for this particular dessert.

SERVES 6

15-30ml (1-2 tablespoons) lemon juice
300ml (½ pint) freshly squeezed orange juice
600ml (1 pint) medium white wine
grated zest of 2 unwaxed lemons
4 whole cloves
125g (4oz) caster sugar

6 ripe pears
75ml (3fl oz) whipping cream
75g (½oz) toasted hazelnuts
For the chocolate sauce
50g (2oz) dark chocolate with 70 per cent cocoa solids
15g (½oz) unsalted butter

- In a large saucepan, put the lemon juice and zest, orange juice, wine, cloves and caster sugar. Heat gently to dissolve the sugar.

- Peel each pear, leaving the stems attached. Slice off the bottom of each pear so it will stand up. Remove the core with a sharp knife. Stand the pears upright in the saucepan. Simmer, covered, for 20 minutes or until the fruit is tender.

- Remove the pears from the saucepan and set aside.

- Remove the cloves from the syrup and discard. Simmer the liquid for about 45 minutes until the syrup is well reduced to about 200ml (7fl oz). The liquid will become much darker and thicker. Leave to cool.

- When the pears have cooled, lay each on its side. Using a small, sharp knife, slit the pears open, leaving the stalks attached. Whip the cream until it holds its shape, then fold in the hazelnuts. Spoon the cream mixture into each pear hollow. Gently put the pears together again and stand upright in a serving dish.

- To prepare the chocolate sauce, gently melt the chocolate and butter together in a small saucepan. Do not boil.

- Pour a little of the syrup over each pear and serve the rest separately. Pour a little of the chocolate sauce over the top of the pears and serve.

APPLE BREAD PUDDING

Budino di Mele

This pudding is made with bread, but I think you get great results by using slices of Fruit Cake Ring. You will find the recipe on page 137.

SERVES 6-8

180g (6oz) caster sugar
75g (3oz) raisins
30-45ml (2-3 tablespoons) brandy
12 slices of day-old bread or cake
350ml (12fl oz) milk

3 large free range, eggs
pinch of salt
75g (3oz) unsalted butter
5 apples

- Put 75g (3oz) of the sugar and 100ml (4fl oz) water in a saucepan. Heat gently until the sugar has dissolved, then bring to the boil and heat for about 5 minutes until it turns to a caramel colour. Immediately, carefully pour the caramel into a 23cm (9 inch) deep ring mould and swirl to coat the bottom of the mould.

- Put the raisins in a small bowl, cover with the brandy and leave to marinate for 30 minutes.

- Put the bread or cake in a large dish and pour over the milk. Set aside.

- Meanwhile, core, peel and thinly slice the apples. In a large bowl, whisk together the remaining sugar with the eggs, salt and butter until well blended. Drain the raisins and add to the sugar mixture with the brandy and the apple slices. Drain the soaked bread, add to the mixture and blend the ingredients together.

- Pre-heat the oven to 180°C, 350°F, Gas Mark 4.

- Pour the apple and bread mixture into the mould, spreading it in evenly. Place the mould in a roasting tin and fill the tin with enough boiling water to come 4cm (1½ inch) up the sides of the mould.

- Bake in the oven for 45 minutes until set. Remove the mould from the tin, let it stand for 2 minutes, then place a serving dish over the top of the mould and carefully invert the pudding onto it. Shake and release the pudding and the sauce. Serve warm, cut into wedges.

LEMON MASCARPONE CHEESECAKE

Torta di Mascarpone
(See colour photograph)

This is always a popular dessert and it is easy to make. It can also be made with ricotta cheese and can be served with fresh strawberries or raspberries, when they are in season.

SERVES 8

75g (3oz) unsalted butter
175g (6oz) Amaretti biscuits
   (almond macaroons)
400g (14oz) mascarpone cheese
grated zest of 3 unwaxed lemons
and juice of 1 lemon
100g (4oz) caster sugar
2 free range eggs, separated
30ml (2 tablespoons) cornflour
pinch of salt

- Pre-heat the oven to 180°C, 350°F, Gas Mark 4. Grease a deep, 20cm (8 inch) loose-bottomed cake tin.

- Melt the butter. Crush the Amaretti biscuits, then mix the crumbs with the melted butter. Put in the bottom of the prepared tin.

- Put the cheese, lemon zest and juice, sugar and egg yolks in a bowl and, using a wooden spoon, mix together. Sprinkle the cornflour over the top and fold in.

- In a separate bowl, whisk the whites with the salt until stiff. Fold into the cheese mixture. Spread the mixture into the cake tin and smooth the top.

- Bake in the oven for 35 minutes until firm to the touch. Leave to cool in the tin.

THE APOSTLES' FINGERS

Dita Degli Apostoli

Please don't be put off by the title. These fingers are carefully rolled pancakes with a fresh ricotta and chocolate filling. When they have been cut they really do resemble fingers.

MAKES 64 FINGERS

For the batter
5 free range eggs
25g (1oz) caster sugar
125g (4oz) plain white or Italian type '00' flour
pinch of salt
225ml (8fl oz) milk
unsalted butter, for greasing
For the filling
450g (1lb) ricotta cheese
175g (6oz) caster sugar

grated zest of 1 unwaxed lemon
grated zest of 1 orange
grated zest of 1 clementine (optional)
15ml (1 tablespoon) double cream
50g (2oz) dark chocolate with 70 per cent cocoa solids
30ml (2 tablespoons) rum
candied zest (see page 204), to decorate (optional)

- To prepare the batter, whisk together the eggs and sugar until well blended. Beat in the flour, add the salt and gradually add the milk, whisking vigorously until the batter is smooth. Cover and leave to stand for 30 minutes-1 hour.

- To make the filling, put the ricotta cheese into a bowl and beat in the sugar, the zests and the cream until smooth. Finely chop the chocolate and beat into the mixture with the rum.

- Wipe a heavy, 28cm (11 inch) non-stick crêpe pan with a little butter. Place over a medium heat. When the pan is medium hot, ladle in enough batter to cover the base. Cook until it bubbles and the underside is golden brown, then turn and cook the other side until golden brown. Remove from the pan and stack on a large plate, interleaved with greaseproof paper. Repeat with the remaining batter to make 8 pancakes.

- Lay a pancake on a work surface and cut away any brittle edges. Place a heaped tablespoon of filling in the middle, then spread very thinly over the whole pancake. Roll the pancake tightly towards you. Repeat with each pancake.

- Slice each across at a slight diagonal into 8 fingers. Discard the ends of each roll. Chill in the fridge before serving.

- If wished, decorate with candied zest and eat with your fingers.

SWEET CHOCOLATE TRIFLE

Zuppa Dolce al Cioccolato

This recipe is more like a very rich chocolate mousse with brandy-soaked biscuits. It's very quick to prepare and tastes even better eaten the next day.

SERVES 8

3 Lady's Fingers (see page 184) or 3 slices of Italian Sponge Cake (see page 129)
30ml (2 tablespoons) brandy
175g (6oz) dark chocolate with 70 per cent cocoa solids
40g (1½oz) unsalted butter
3 free range eggs, separated
75g (3oz) caster sugar
60ml (4 tablespoons) double cream
toasted, flaked almonds, for decorating

- Lay the Lady's Fingers or Italian Sponge Cake in the bottom of a 20cm (8 inch) shallow, round serving dish. Pour over the brandy and leave to soak.

- Meanwhile, melt together the chocolate and butter and leave to cool.

- Whisk together the egg yolks and sugar until thick and creamy and add to the chocolate mixture. Whip the cream until stiff and fold into the chocolate mixture. Whisk the egg whites until stiff and fold into the chocolate mixture.

- Pour into the serving dish. Chill for 2-3 hours or up to 1 day in the fridge before serving, decorated with toasted almonds.

COFFEE RICOTTA

Ricotta al Caffè

Ricotta is a favourite ingredient of mine. I like its many uses in both sweet and savoury dishes. It is a by-product of cheese-making and is made from the whey. Ricotta varies in flavour depending on whether full-cream or skimmed milk is added. I love its cool and creamy texture and I'm addicted to coffee so this is a real favourite for me.

SERVES 4

275g (10oz) ricotta cheese
100g (4oz) golden caster sugar
30ml (2 tablespoon) finely-ground coffee
30ml (2 tablespoons) rum

5ml (1 teaspoon) vanilla extract
double cream and Twice Baked Cookies (see page 178), to serve

- Sieve the ricotta cheese into a bowl. Add the remaining ingredients and stir together until smooth.

- Place in a serving dish and leave in the fridge for at least 2½ hours for the flavour to develop.

- Serve with fresh cream and cookies.

FRIED APPLE SLICES

Mele Fritte

This is a dessert from the region of Emilia-Romagna. It is an ideal recipe to make when apples are in season and I prefer to use Cox's orange pippins or Braeburn apples. My grandmother used to marinate the apples in a little brandy.

SERVES 4

7g (¼ teaspoon) fresh yeast or 5ml (1 teaspoon) dried yeast
100ml (4fl oz) hand-hot water
125g (4oz) caster sugar
1 large free range egg, beaten
45ml (3 tablespoons) olive oil

100ml (4fl oz) dry white wine
225g (8oz) plain white or Italian type '00' flour
1.25ml (¼ teaspoon) salt
4 eating apples
300ml (½ pt) olive oil, for frying

- Cream the fresh yeast with the water. (If using dried yeast, sprinkle it into the water with a pinch of the sugar and leave in a warm place for 15 minutes until frothy.) Add 30ml (2 tablespoons) of the sugar, the egg, olive oil and wine and blend well together.

- Put the flour and salt into a large bowl. Make a well in the centre, add the yeast mixture and beat with a whisk until it is like a pancake batter. If the batter seems too stiff, add a little more wine or water.

- Peel, core and slice each apple into 5 rings. In a deep, heavy-based saucepan, heat the olive oil. Coat a few apple slices on both sides with the batter, letting the excess drain off. Fry the slices for 3-4 minutes until golden brown. Drain on kitchen paper. Cook the remaining apple slices in the same way.

- Put the remaining sugar on a plate. When the apple slices are cool enough to handle, gently press them into the sugar. Serve warm.

RUM BABA

Baba al Rhum

This recipe is dedicated to my grandpa and father, who both relish this dessert. It is typical of Naples, where you can even buy them in small jars, but they are so much better freshly made. To make individual Rum Babas, you can use muffin cases.

SERVES 8-12

For the baba mixture
50ml (2fl oz) milk
25g (1oz) unsalted butter
25g (1oz) fresh yeast or 15ml (1 tablespoon) dried
2 egg yolks plus 1 egg
50g (2oz) caster sugar
5ml (1 teaspoon) vanilla extract
grated zest of 1 unwaxed lemon

50g (2oz) raisins
225g (8oz) strong white flour
For the rum sauce
125g (4oz) caster sugar
2 slices of unwaxed lemon
1 slice of orange
1 cinnamon stick
50ml (2fl oz) dark rum

- Grease a deep, round 20cm (8 inch) cake tin.

- Gently heat the milk and butter until the butter has melted. Remove from the heat and leave to cool until hand-hot. Cream the fresh yeast with 30ml (2 tablespoons) of the warm milk mixture.

- Mix together the egg yolks and sugar until thick and creamy, then add the egg, vanilla extract, lemon zest, raisins, flour and the yeast mixture. Mix well with a wooden spoon. Place in an oiled bowl and cover with a clean tea-towel.

- Leave to rise in a warm place for 1½-2 hours until doubled in size.

- Turn out onto a lightly floured surface and knead lightly until smooth. Place in the prepared tin and leave in a warm place for about 45 minutes until the mixture fills about two-thirds of the tin.

- Pre-heat the oven to 180°C, 350°F, Gas Mark 4.

- Bake in the oven for 20-25 minutes until golden brown and well risen. Leave to cool in the tin for 5 minutes, then turn out and cool on a wire rack.

- Meanwhile, make the rum sauce. Place all the ingredients and 200ml (7fl oz) water in a saucepan, bring to the boil and simmer for 8 minutes. Leave to cool, then strain. Set aside to pour over the cake.

- When the cake is cooked and still warm, pour over the rum sauce. Leave to soak for 1½ hours before serving.

SICILIAN ORANGES

Arance alla Siciliana

Sicilians have some of the best recipes for oranges. This is one that is enjoyed throughout Italy.

SERVES 6

6 oranges
50ml (2fl oz) brandy
4 cloves

525g (1lb 3oz) sugar
1 cinnamon stick

- Using a sharp knife or vegetable peeler, cut 10 long, thin strips of zest from the oranges. Then cut the zest into smaller strips. Blanch the strips in boiling water, return to the boil then drain and reserve the liquid in a measuring jug.

- Remove and discard the remaining peel and the pith from the oranges. Place the oranges in a bowl with the brandy, cloves, 75g (3oz) of the sugar and the cinnamon. Cover and leave in the fridge overnight.

- To make the syrup, put the remaining 450g (1lb) sugar and 175ml (6fl oz) of the reserved water in a saucepan and cook over a medium heat, stirring constantly, until the sugar dissolves. Bring to the boil and continue to cook, without stirring, until light golden.

- Arrange the oranges on a serving dish, drizzle over the syrup and top with the strips of orange zest.

MONT BLANC

Monte Bianco

Mont Blanc is one of the highest peaks in the Alps and in this recipe the chestnut mixture falls like snow to represent the mountain. This dessert can be served as an accompaniment to meringues.

SERVES 8

700g (1½lbs) fresh chestnuts or two 425g (15oz) cans of whole chestnuts, drained
5ml (1 teaspoon) salt

125g (4oz) caster sugar
300ml (½ pint) double cream
icing sugar and cocoa powder, for dusting

- If using fresh chestnuts, pierce each chestnut and put in a saucepan of water with the salt. Bring to the boil and cook for 25 minutes. Drain and, as soon as they are cool enough to handle, remove the shells and skin.

- Put the fresh or canned chestnuts in a large bowl and mash with a fork. Gradually mix in the caster sugar.

- Pass the chestnut mixture through a potato ricer or food mill to form shreds of mixture, directly into a serving dish. Make sure it falls like snow and forms into a dome shape.

- Whip the cream until it just holds its shape and put on top of the chestnut mixture. Chill in the fridge for 3 hours.

- Before serving, sprinkle with sifted icing sugar and cocoa powder.

MRS FERRIGNO'S MERINGUES

Meringa Ferrigno

My mother makes the best meringues I've ever tasted. They are crisp on the outside and chewy inside. My mother will say it's the Aga that produces such good results. I know it's because she is so particular at every stage of making them. Meringues are popular in Italy, eaten plain, with fruit or cream.

MAKES 10 FILLED MERINGUES OR 6 NESTS

4 large egg whites, at room temperature	225g (8oz) caster sugar
pinch of salt	double cream, to serve
	fresh fruit, to serve (optional)

- Pre-heat the oven to 150°C, 300°F, Gas Mark 2. Line 2 or more baking trays with baking parchment.

- In a large, clean bowl, whisk together the egg whites and salt until thick and creamy. Add half the sugar and continue whisking. Gradually fold in the remaining sugar. The mixture should be very stiff and opaque.

- Form individual nests or rounds on to the prepared trays. Bake in the oven for 1½ hours until dry. Turn over and bake for a further 45 minutes. They will have changed colour and become deep golden. Leave to cool on a wire rack.

- To serve, either sandwich the meringues with whipped cream or make into fruit-filled nests with cream.

ZUCCOTTO

This traditional Tuscan dessert is recognised by the classical pattern of the icing sugar and cocoa decoration. It is particularly good when served the day after it's made. Keep in the fridge until served.

SERVES 10-12

275g (10oz) dark chocolate with 70 per cent cocoa solids
75g (3oz) toasted blanched almonds
75g (3oz) toasted blanched hazelnuts
1 litre (1¾ pints) whipping cream
150g (5oz) icing sugar

45ml (3 tablespoons) rum
45ml (3 tablespoons) brandy
45ml (3 tablespoons) cherry brandy
½ an Italian Sponge Cake, cut horizontally (see page 129)
2 tablespoons cocoa powder

- Line a 1.7 litre (3 pint) pudding basin with a circle of greaseproof paper and lightly grease with oil.

- Break half of the chocolate into a heatproof bowl and stand the bowl over a saucepan of simmering water. Heat until melted then remove the bowl from the heat. Chop the remaining chocolate into small pieces.

- Roughly chop the almonds and hazelnuts. Whip the cream until it holds its shape, then mix in the chopped nuts and chocolate.

- Divide the cream in half and add the melted chocolate to one half. Sift 50g (2oz) of icing sugar into each half of the cream and stir in gently. Chill in the fridge until required. Slice the crust off the top of the cake half. Push the cake into the bowl and ease it to line the sides.

- Mix together the rum, brandy and cherry brandy. Brush the cake with the rum mixture to moisten it completely and help it to fit the bowl firmly. Trim off any untidy edges and use your hands to get as smooth a finish as possible.

- Spoon in the white cream mixture and spread it evenly up the sides. Fill the centre with the chocolate mixture and smooth the top.

- Place in the fridge for at least 2 hours before serving.

- Cut out a circle of greaseproof paper about the same size as the Zuccotto when turned out. Draw on it 8 even slices and cut out each alternate slice. Mix together the cocoa powder and remaining icing sugar.

- To serve, turn out the Zuccotto onto a serving plate. Place the cut-out paper over the Zuccotto and liberally sift the sugar mixture on top. Carefully remove the paper and you will have adorned the Zuccotto with its classical design.

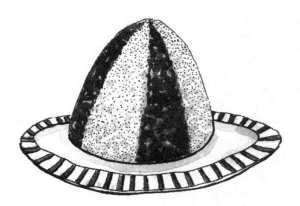

HOT FRUIT POACHED IN AN ORANGE AND GRAND MARNIER SAUCE

Affogata di Frutta al Grand Marnier

This recipe is a speciality of my friend, Claudio, who has a restaurant in Perugia called 'La Taverna'. It is so simple, yet so delicious. Be sure to use fresh fruit and instead of Grand Marnier, other orange-flavoured liqueurs can be used, such as Cointreau or Mandarine Napoleon.

SERVES 8-10

900g (2lb) fresh fruit in season, such as ripe pears, nectarines, pineapple, cherries, seedless grapes
150g (5oz) unsalted butter

1 unwaxed lemon
225g (8oz) caster sugar
juice of 8 oranges
45-60ml (3-4 tablespoons) Grand Marnier

- Prepare the fruit, peeling, stoning and cutting it into bite-sized pieces.

- Melt the butter in a large saucepan. While it is melting, use a zester to remove the zest from the lemon. Reserve some for decoration and add the rest to the pan. Stir in the sugar. Keep stirring quickly as the sauce heats and starts to bubble gently.

- Cook for about 10 minutes, stirring all the time. After about 8-10 minutes it will become pale and fudge-like in appearance. Remove the pan from the heat.

- Pour the orange juice into a measuring jug and make up to 450ml (15fl oz) with water. Slowly pour the orange juice into the pan, otherwise it will spit and bubble. (Do not worry if the caramel goes hard.) Return the pan to the heat and heat gently until it dissolves. Return to the boil and continue to boil gently for a further 2 or 3 minutes.

- Meanwhile, strain the juice from ½ the lemon. Add the Grand Marnier and lemon juice to the sauce. Taste and, if preferred, add more liqueur, or a little more lemon juice.

- Add the prepared fruit adding the grapes last of all, if used, and bring to simmering point. Serve hot, in a warmed serving bowl, scattered with the reserved lemon zest.

PEACHES AND STRAWBERRIES IN MARSALA

Pesche Fragole al Marsala

In Italy we have many different fruits to make the perfect ending to a meal. Sometimes the fruit is simply served bobbing in a bowl of water, for you to peel and eat. This dessert is more sophisticated and can be eaten when both fruits are at their best.

SERVES 4

2 ripe medium peaches	15ml (1 tablespoon) icing sugar
225g (8oz) ripe strawberries	(optional)
	60ml (4 tablespoons) Marsala

- Skin the peaches, remove the stones and slice the flesh. Remove the stems from the strawberries, wipe and slice in half.

- In a bowl, gently mix together the peaches and strawberries, the sugar if using, and the wine. Cover and leave to marinate for 1 hour.

- Serve in individual glass dishes and accompany with plain sweet biscuits.

Perfect Pastries and Tarts

This was one of my favourite chapters to write. I love Italian pastry, pasta frolla, which is crisp and buttery, encasing a delicious, fragrant filling. Fig and Lemon Tart is a real star recipe for me, as is Pine Kernel Tart, which is eaten throughout Italy. Individual pastries have not been forgotten. These include Chocolate Nut Pastries and Honey and Spice Twists. Savouring a pastry with a strong cup of espresso coffee is one of the great pleasures of Italian life.

APRICOT AND ALMOND TART

Torta di Albicocche e Mandorle
(See colour photograph)

My mother and grandmother have passed on to me their love of apricots. Their bright orange flesh is irresistible to eat, either on their own or in this tart.

SERVES 8

225g (8oz) plain white or Italian type '00' flour
pinch of salt
25g (1oz) cornflour
125g (4oz) plus 10ml (2 teaspoons) icing sugar
125g (4oz) unsalted butter
2 free range eggs and 1 egg yolk

8 ripe apricots
75g (3oz) ground almonds
grated zest and juice of 1 unwaxed lemon
25g (1oz) flaked almonds
icing sugar, for dusting
cream, to serve (optional)

- Pre-heat the oven to 200°C, 400°F, Gas Mark 6.

- Sift the flour, salt, cornflour and the 10 ml (2 teaspoons) of icing sugar into a bowl. Rub in the butter until the mixture resembles breadcrumbs. Add the egg yolk and 30ml (2 tablespoons) of cold water and mix to bind the ingredients together. Knead very lightly.

- On a lightly floured surface, roll out the dough and use to line a 23cm (9 inch) fluted, loose-bottomed flan tin. Chill in the fridge for 20 minutes.

- Line the pastry case with greaseproof paper and weigh down with baking beans. Bake in the oven for 15 minutes until the sides are crisp. Remove the lining and beans and return to the oven for 5 minutes until the bottom is crisp.

- Put the 125g (4oz) icing sugar, the 2 eggs, ground almonds and lemon zest and juice in a bowl and mix well together. Pour into the flan case.

- Cut the apricots in half, remove the stones, then arrange in the flan case with the skin side down. Sprinkle over the flaked almonds.

- Bake in the oven for about 35 minutes until the filling is firm and golden. Dust with sifted icing sugar. Serve hot or cold, with cream if wished.

DRIED PEACH AND LEMON TART

Crostata di Pesche e Limone

This is a fusion of my favourite flavours – dried peaches and delicious, tangy lemons. The pastry can be made in a food processor for convenience.

SERVES 10-12

For the pastry
225g (8oz) plain white or Italian type '00' flour
pinch of salt
75g (3oz) icing sugar
100g (4oz) unsalted butter
1 large free range egg
a few drops of vanilla extract
grated zest of 1 unwaxed lemon
For the filling
grated zest and juice of 4 unwaxed lemons
100g (4oz) unsalted butter
100g (4oz) caster sugar
4 large free range eggs, lightly beaten
275g (10oz) no-soak dried peaches
5ml (1 teaspoon) almond extract
For the topping
225ml (8fl oz) double cream
a few mint leaves, for decorating

- To make the pastry, sift the flour, salt and icing sugar into a bowl, then rub in the butter until the mixture resembles breadcrumbs. Make a well in the centre, add the egg, vanilla extract and lemon zest and gradually mix in the flour from the edges to form a smooth dough.

- Wrap the pastry in greaseproof paper and leave to rest in the fridge for 30 minutes.

- Pre-heat the oven to 200°C, 400°F, Gas Mark 6.

- On a lightly floured surface, roll out the dough and use to line a 28 (11 inch) loose-bottomed flan tin. With a fork, prick the base all over. Line with greaseproof paper and weigh down with baking beans.

- Bake in the oven for about 15 minutes until the sides of the pastry are crisp. Remove the lining and beans and return to the oven for 5 minutes until the bottom is crisp. Remove from the tin and leave to cool.

- To make the filling, put the lemon zest and juice, the butter and three quarters of the sugar in a medium saucepan and heat gently, stirring with a wooden spoon until the butter melts. Stir in the eggs and cook over a medium heat until the mixture thickens and coats the back of the spoon. (Do not allow the mixture to boil or the eggs will curdle.) Remove from the heat and leave to cool.

- Put the dried peaches and 225ml (8fl oz) water with the remaining sugar in a pan and simmer for about 5 minutes until soft.

- Turn the peaches into a food processor, add the almond extract and blend to form a purée. Leave to cool.

- Spread the lemon mixture in the tart case, then add the peach mixture. Chill in the fridge for at least 1 hour before serving.

- To serve, whip the cream until it holds its shape and pipe on top of the tart. Decorate with mint leaves.

CHOCOLATE PEAR TART

Crostata di Pere a Cioccolato

This is inspired by the pear harvest in Italy. Although perhaps unusual in a tart, I just love this combination.

SERVES 8-12

For the pastry
50g (2oz) unsalted butter
100g (4oz) plain white or Italian
  type '00' flour
25g (1oz) cocoa powder
50g (2oz) caster sugar
1 free range egg, beaten

For the filling
45ml (3 tablespoons) orange
  marmalade
2 ripe pears
100g (4oz) dark chocolate with 70
  per cent cocoa solids
50g (2oz) unsalted butter
2 free range eggs, separated
100g (4oz) caster sugar

- To make the pastry, rub the butter into the flour until the mixture resembles breadcrumbs. Sift in the cocoa powder, add the sugar and enough of the beaten egg to bind the mixture together. Knead lightly, wrap in greaseproof paper and chill in the fridge for 20 minutes.

- Pre-heat the oven to 180°C, 350°F, Gas Mark 4.

- On a lightly floured surface, roll out the pastry and use to line a 20cm (8 inch) flan tin. Cover the bottom with the marmalade.

- Peel the pears, cut into quarters and remove the cores. Arrange them in the flan case.

- To make the filling, melt the chocolate and butter over a low heat. Set aside to cool.

- Beat together the egg yolks and sugar until pale and fluffy. Fold in the chocolate mixture. Whisk the egg whites until stiff, then fold into the mixture.

- Pour the mixture over the pears and bake in the oven for 40 minutes until firm to the touch. Serve hot or cold.

GRANDMOTHER'S PIE

Torta Della Nonna

On a whistle-stop tour of Florence, in search of some interesting breads, I came across this pie and enjoyed a piece for breakfast with an espresso. What a wonderful start to my morning! There are many regional varieties of this pie.

SERVES 15

For the pastry
450g (1lb) plain white or Italian type '00' flour
10ml (2 teaspoons) baking powder
pinch of salt
225g (8oz) unsalted butter
175g (6oz) caster sugar
15ml (1 tablespoon) milk
10ml (2 teaspoons) vanilla extract
1 large free range egg
For the filling
300ml (½ pint) milk

100g (4oz) semolina flour
450g (1lb) ricotta cheese
2 large free range eggs
100g (4oz) granulated sugar
grated zest of 2 large oranges
juice of 1 orange
To finish
60ml (4 tablespoons) apricot conserve
175g (6oz) toasted, slivered almonds
icing sugar, for dusting

- Pre-heat the oven to 190°C, 375°F, Gas Mark 5.

- To make the pastry, sift the flour, baking powder and salt into a large bowl, then rub in the butter until the mixture resembles fine breadcrumbs. Stir in the sugar.

- To make the filling, pour the milk into a medium saucepan, and heat until warm. Stir in the semolina in a thin stream and continue to stir the mixture until it thickens and leaves the sides of the pan. Remove from the heat and leave to cool slightly.

- In a large bowl, mix together the ricotta cheese, eggs, sugar, orange zest and juice. Add the semolina mixture and, using an electric mixer, beat until blended.

- In a small bowl, lightly whisk together the milk, vanilla and egg, then mix into the flour mixture. With your hands, combine together to form a soft ball of dough.

- Divide the dough in half. On a lightly floured surface, roll one half into a 38x29cm (15x11½ inch) rectangle. Place the dough on a greased baking tray. Spread the filling evenly over the dough to the edges.

- Roll the remaining dough into a 38x29cm (15x11½ inch) rectangle. Using your rolling pin, carefully lift the dough and place it over the filling. Using a fork, pinch the edges together.

- Bake in the oven for 30-35 minutes until golden. Whilst the pie is still warm, brush with apricot conserve and sprinkle with almonds to decorate. Leave to cool.

- Before serving, sprinkle the pie with sifted icing sugar.

PEACH AND MASCARPONE TART

Crostata di Pesche e Mascarpone

This delicious tart is enjoyed in Sicily when the peaches are ripe. The pastry is a dream!

SERVES 8

For the pastry
150g (5oz) plain white or Italian type '00' flour
50g (2oz) icing sugar
45ml (3 tablespoons) ground almonds
2.5ml (½ teaspoon) baking powder
pinch of salt
125g (4oz) chilled unsalted butter
1 free range egg, beaten

For the filling
250g (8oz) mascarpone cheese
50g (2oz) icing sugar
grated zest of 1orange
5ml (1 teaspoon) vanilla extract
125g (4fl oz) double cream
4 large, ripe peaches
45ml (3 tablespoons) apricot conserve

- To make the pastry, mix together the flour, icing sugar, almonds, baking powder and salt in a large bowl. Rub in the butter until the mixture resembles fine breadcrumbs. Add the egg and mix to form a smooth dough.

- On a lightly floured surface, roll out the dough and use to line a 24cm (9½ inch) loose-bottomed tin. Chill in the fridge for 30 minutes.

- Pre-heat the oven to 180°C, 350°F, Gas Mark 4.

- Line the pastry case with greaseproof paper and weigh down with baking beans. Bake in the oven for 15-20 minutes until the sides of the pastry are crisp. Remove the lining and beans and return to the oven for a further 5 minutes until golden brown. Leave to cool.

- To make the filling, mix the mascarpone cheese, icing sugar, orange zest and vanilla extract in a bowl. Whip the cream until it just holds its shape, then fold into the mascarpone cheese mixture.

- Peel, stone and thinly slice the peaches. Spread the filling mixture in the pastry case and top with the peach slices. Melt the apricot conserve and brush over the peach slices to glaze. Chill in the fridge for 1 hour before serving.

HONEY AND SPICE TWISTS

Zeppole

These are traditionally eaten on Christmas eve – a huge pyramid of golden, light pastries, smothered in honey and mixed spice. My grandmother used to rise early on Christmas Eve especially to make them. They are delicious, but take a bit of practice to make perfectly.

SERVES 4-5

15g (½oz) fresh yeast or 7.5ml (1½ teaspoons) dried yeast and a pinch of sugar
150ml (¼ pint) hand-hot water
225g (8oz) plain white or Italian type '00' flour
pinch of salt
1 free range egg, beaten
olive oil, for deep frying
caster sugar, for dusting
10ml (2 teaspoons) mixed spice
45ml (3 tablespoons) honey

- Blend the fresh yeast with 30ml (2 tablespoons) of the hand-hot water. If using dried yeast, sprinkle it into 30ml (2 tablespoons) of the water with the sugar, and leave in a warm place for 15 minutes until frothy.

- Sift the flour and salt into a large bowl and make a well in the centre.

- Pour the yeast liquid, beaten egg and some of the remaining water into the centre and mix together, gradually adding the remaining water, to form a dough.

- Turn the dough on to a well floured surface and knead for 10 minutes until smooth.

- Put the dough in a lightly oiled bowl, cover with a clean tea-towel and leave to rest for 20 minutes.

- Take a large chestnut-sized piece of dough and roll into a thin sausage-shape, then cross the ends over to form a loop at one end. Continue with the dough to make 15 Zeppole.

- Heat the olive oil in a saucepan. Cook 5 pieces of dough at a time. When they bob to the surface, drain on kitchen paper.

- When all the dough is cooked, dust with caster sugar and the mixed spice. Pile the Zeppole into a pyramid on a serving plate.

- Heat the honey in a small saucepan, then pour over the top of the Zeppole. Serve on the same day that you make them.

CHOCOLATE NUT PASTRIES

Rotolo di Cioccolato e Noci

I first enjoyed these in Florence, then started making them myself. They are simple to make, yet look and taste wonderful.

MAKES 12

200g (7oz) plain white or Italian type '00' flour
pinch of salt
125g (5oz) unsalted butter
150g (5oz) caster sugar
1 free range egg, beaten

150g (5oz) dark chocolate with 70 per cent cocoa solids
10ml (2 teaspoons) ground cinnamon
100g (4oz) chopped hazelnuts

- To make the pastry, put the flour and salt into a bowl and rub in 75g (3oz) of the butter until the mixture resembles breadcrumbs. Stir in the sugar. Add the beaten egg and use to bind the mixture together. Wrap in greaseproof paper and chill in the fridge for 30 minutes.

- Meanwhile, make the filling. Melt together the chocolate and remaining 50g (2oz) butter then stir in the cinnamon and hazelnuts. Set to one side to cool.

- Pre-heat the oven to 190°C, 375°F, Gas Mark 5.

- On a lightly floured surface, roll out the pastry to a 30x20cm (12x8 inch) rectangle, making sure that you can lift up the pastry. Spread over the cooled chocolate mixture and roll up lengthways to form a Swiss roll.

- Cut carefully into 12 slices and place, cut side down, on baking trays.

- Bake in the oven for 15-20 minutes until the pastry is golden. Leave to cool on the baking trays before serving.

GARIBALDI PASTRIES

Biscotti di Garibaldi

These are eaten all over Italy. They are blissfully straightforward to make and children just love them.

MAKES 24

100g (4oz) plain white or Italian type '00' flour
75g (3oz) unsalted butter
50g (2oz) caster sugar plus a little

extra, to finish
100g (4oz) currants
1 large free range egg, beaten

- Pre-heat the oven to 180°C, 350°F, Gas Mark 4. Lightly grease a 30x20cm (12x8 inch) Swiss roll tin.

- Sift the flour into a mixing bowl. Add the butter, cut into pieces, and rub it into the flour until it is evenly distributed and the mixture resembles fine breadcrumbs. Stir in the sugar and currants.

- Add almost all the beaten egg to bind the ingredients together and form a soft but not sticky dough.

- Turn the dough into the prepared tin and roll it out so that the base is evenly covered and the surface is smooth.

- Brush the remaining egg over the dough and sprinkle the top with the extra caster sugar.

- Bake in the oven for about 20 minutes until golden brown. As soon as the pastries are cooked, cut them into 24 triangles. Transfer to a wire rack and leave to cool.

FIG AND LEMON TART

Crostata di Fichi e Limoni

This tart is best made with the madonna fig, which is the first fig of the year, picked at the end of May. You will find the tart is very moist and so ideally eaten on the day it is made.

SERVES 10-12

225g (8oz) plain white or Italian
   type '00' flour
5ml (1 teaspoon) vanilla extract
225g (8oz) caster sugar
100g (4oz) unsalted butter

1 egg yolk
5ml (1 teaspoon) salt
6 unwaxed lemons
1kg (2¼ lbs) fresh figs, washed
5ml (1 teaspoon) fennel seeds

- To make the pastry, put the flour in a bowl and make a well in the centre. Add the vanilla extract, half the sugar, the butter, egg yolk and salt and mix well together to form a dough. Wrap in greaseproof paper and chill in the fridge for 20 minutes.

- Using a skewer, prick the skins of the lemons well. Put in a saucepan, add enough water to just cover, bring to the boil and boil for 10 minutes. Repeat this boiling process 3 times, changing the water each time.

- Drain the lemons, reserving the water. Finely slice the lemons, leaving on the skin. Put the lemon slices in a saucepan with the remaining sugar and the reserved water. Cover and cook over a low heat for about 10 minutes until the liquid has reduced to about 150ml (¼ pint) and is syrupy. Drain off the syrup and reserve.

- Pre-heat the oven to 180°C, 350°F, Gas Mark 4.

- On the lightly floured surface, roll out the pastry and use to line a 28cm (11 inch) flan tin. Cover the dough with the lemon slices. Slice the figs and arrange on top. Pour the lemon syrup over the figs and sprinkle with the fennel seeds. Bake in the oven for 45 minutes until the pastry is golden. Leave to cool before serving.

BAKED SWEET PASTRIES

Minni di Santa Agatha

These small, dome-shaped pastries are made from sweet pasta dough. Their shape has inspired the name which, literally translated, means breasts of Saint Agatha.

MAKES ABOUT 12

For the pastry
225g (8oz) plain white or Italian type '00' flour
65g (2½oz) caster sugar
100g (4oz) unsalted butter
1 free range egg
5ml (1 teaspoon) finely grated lemon zest
pinch of salt
cocoa powder and icing sugar, for dusting

For the filling
15ml (1 tablespoon) toasted hazelnuts
15ml (1 tablespoon) candied orange peel or mixed peel
25g (1oz) dark chocolate with 50 per cent solids
225g (8oz) ricotta cheese
50g (2oz) caster sugar
7.5ml (1½ teaspoons) vanilla extract
1 egg yolk

- To make the pastry, put the flour and sugar into a food processor and, working on full speed, add the butter in pieces until well mixed. With the food processor still running, add the egg, lemon zest and salt. Turn the dough onto greaseproof paper, flatten, cover and chill in the fridge for 30 minutes.

- For the filling, finely chop the hazelnuts and orange peel and grate the chocolate. Push the ricotta through a sieve into a bowl. Stir in the sugar, vanilla extract, egg yolk, peel, hazelnuts and chocolate until mixed.

- Remove the pastry from the fridge and allow to come to room temperature.

- Pre-heat the oven to 180°C, 350°F, Gas Mark 4. Grease a large baking tray.

- Divide the pastry in half and, on a lightly floured surface, roll out each half to a narrow strip measuring 15x56cm (6x22 inch). Arrange heaped teaspoonfuls of the filling in two rows along one of the pastry strips, ensuring that there is at least a 2.5cm (1 inch) space around each spoonful. Brush the pastry between the filling with beaten egg. Carefully place the second strip of pastry on top and press down gently between each mound of filling to seal.

- Using a plain, round cutter, cut each covered mound of filling to make circular parcels. Lift each parcel and, with your fingers, gently seal the edges.

- Place each pastry on the prepared baking tray and bake in the oven for 15 minutes until lightly golden. Serve warm, dusted with sifted cocoa powder and icing sugar.

NEAPOLITAN RICOTTA TART

Pastiera Napoletana

This recipe comes from the Cappuccino Convent at Amalfi. It is rich and I think it is good eaten the day after it is made.

SERVES 10

For the pastry
225g (8oz) unsalted butter
175g (6oz) caster sugar
4 egg yolks
450g (1 lb) plain white or Italian type '00' flour

For the filling
450g (1lb) ricotta cheese
100g (4oz) caster sugar
5ml (1 teaspoon) ground cinnamon

grated zest and juice of 1 unwaxed lemon
60ml (4 tablespoons) orange flower water
100g (4oz) candied orange or mixed peel
1 free range egg, separated
550ml (scant 1 pint) milk
100g (4oz) vermicelli
large pinch of salt
icing sugar, for dusting

- To make the pastry, put the butter and sugar in a bowl and cream together. Add the egg yolks and then gradually add the flour, mixing well to make a soft dough. Wrap in greaseproof paper and chill in the fridge for 30 minutes.

- To make the filling, put the ricotta cheese, the sugar, reserving 30ml (2 tablespoons), the cinnamon, half the lemon zest, the lemon juice, orange flower water, candied peel and the egg yolk in a bowl and beat together.

- In a small saucepan, bring the milk to the boil, add the vermicelli, remaining 30ml (2 tablespoons) sugar, remaining lemon zest and the salt and simmer gently until the vermicelli has absorbed all the milk. Whilst still warm, blend the pasta carefully into the ricotta mixture.

- Whisk the egg white until it just holds its shape, then fold into the mixture.

- Pre-heat the oven to 190°C, 375°F, Gas Mark 5.

- On a lightly floured surface, roll out the pastry and use two-thirds to line a 28cm (11 inch) loose-bottomed flan tin.

- Add the ricotta filling. Cut the remaining pastry into strips and arrange in a lattice pattern on top of the tart.

- Bake in the oven for 40-50 minutes until golden. Dust with sifted icing sugar before serving warm or cold.

SICILIAN LEMON TART

Torta di Limone Siciliana

This refreshing, tangy tart comes from Sicily. It is so good that you will be sure to want a second slice – fortunately it is large enough to go round.

SERVES 8

200g (7oz) plain white or Italian type '00' flour
75g (3oz) icing sugar plus extra, for dusting
pinch of salt
100g (4oz) unsalted butter

1 small and 3 large free range eggs
5 unwaxed lemons
100g (4oz) caster sugar
50g (2oz) ground almonds
150ml (¼ pint) double cream

- To make the pastry, sift the flour, icing sugar and salt into a bowl. Rub in the butter until the mixture resembles breadcrumbs. Beat the small egg, make a well in the centre of the flour and add the egg and the grated zest of 1 lemon. Gradually work the flour in from the edges and mix to a smooth dough. Wrap in greaseproof paper and leave to rest in the fridge for about 30 minutes before using.

- Pre-heat the oven to 200°C, 400°F, Gas Mark 6.

- On a lightly floured surface, roll out the pastry and use it to line a 28cm (11 inch) flan ring. Do not remove any overhang. Prick the base.

- Put the tin on a baking tray, line the pastry case with greaseproof paper and weigh down with baking beans. Bake in the oven for about 15 minutes until the sides of the pastry are crisp. Remove the lining and beans and trim the edges. Return to the oven for 5 minutes until the bottom is crisp.

- Meanwhile, make the filling. Finely grate the zest of 2 lemons and squeeze out the juice from all of the lemons. In a large bowl, beat the large eggs with the caster sugar until the mixture is thick and pale and leaves a trail when the beaters are lifted. Stir in the lemon rind and juice with the almonds and cream.

- Pour the filling into the baked pastry case. Return to the oven at 180°C, 350°F, Gas Mark 4 and bake for about 40 minutes until softly set.

- Leave until cold, then dust with sifted icing sugar before serving.

INDIVIDUAL FRESH FRUIT TARTLETS

Crostatine di Frutta Fresca

There is something very appealing about little tartlets filled with pastry cream and topped with fresh fruit. Choose small fruits and berries when they come into season.

SERVES 12

For the pastry
350g (12oz) plain white or Italian type '00' flour
175g (6oz) unsalted butter, softened
175g (6oz) caster sugar
grated zest of 1 unwaxed lemon
120ml (8 tablespoons) white rum
pinch of salt
For the pastry cream
3 free range eggs
75g (3oz) caster sugar
40g (1½oz) cornflour
450ml (¾ pint) milk
10ml (2 teaspoons) vanilla extract
For the filling
Fresh fruits in season, such as strawberries, raspberries, figs, grapes, peaches, apricots
For the glaze
60ml (4 tablespoons) apricot conserve
15ml (1 tablespoon) white rum

- To make the pastry, put the flour in a bowl and rub in the butter until the mixture resembles breadcrumbs. Make a well in the centre and add the sugar, lemon zest, rum and salt. Using a fork, mix together to form a ball. Wrap in greaseproof paper and chill in the fridge for 1 hour.

- To make the pastry cream, beat together the eggs and sugar until pale and thick. Sift in the cornflour and beat until smooth. Heat the milk in a saucepan until almost boiling, then pour onto the egg mixture, stirring all the time. Return the mixture to the pan and cook over a low heat, stirring, until the mixture boils. Add the vanilla extract. Cover the surface with a piece of greaseproof paper and leave the mixture to cool completely.

- On a lightly floured surface, roll out the pastry and cut out rounds and use to line twelve 10cm (4 inch) tartlet tins. Line the pastry cases with greaseproof paper and weigh down with baking beans. Chill in the fridge for at least 15 minutes.

- Pre-heat the oven to 180°C, 350°F, Gas Mark 4.

- Bake the tartlets in the oven for 10 minutes, then remove the beans and continue baking for a further 5 minutes until crisp. Transfer to a wire rack and leave to cool.

- Fill the tartlets with the pastry cream and top with whole fruit, or slices of fresh fruit. Sieve the apricot conserve into a saucepan and add the rum. Heat gently, then brush the glaze over the top of the fruit. Serve within 2 hours.

RASPBERRY AND ALMOND TART

Crostata di Lampone

This tart is rich and succulent, with the raspberries enclosed in crisp pastry.

SERVES 8-12

For the pastry
100g (4oz) plain white or Italian type '00' flour
75g (3oz) unsalted butter, chilled and cubed
75g (3oz) caster sugar
5ml (1 teaspoon) ground cinnamon
grated zest of 1 unwaxed lemon
75g (3oz) ground almonds
2 egg yolks, beaten
1 egg white
For the filling
120ml (8 tablespoons) raspberry conserve
225g (8oz) fresh or frozen raspberries
a little caster sugar

- To make the pastry, sift the flour into a large bowl. Add the butter and rub in with your fingertips until the mixture resembles fine breadcrumbs. Stir in the sugar, cinnamon, lemon zest and ground almonds. Stir in the egg yolks and mix with a round-bladed knife until the mixture binds together. Gather the mixture with one hand to form a smooth dough. Wrap in greaseproof paper and chill in the fridge for 1 hour.

- Pre-heat the oven to 180°C, 350°F, Gas Mark 4.

- On a lightly floured surface, roll out the pastry and use to line a 23cm (9 inch) loose-bottomed flan tin. Roll the rolling pin over the edge of the tin to remove excess pastry. Line with greaseproof paper and weigh down with baking beans. Bake in the oven for about 15 minutes until the sides of the pastry are crisp. Remove the lining and beans. Lightly beat the egg white and brush a little over the base of the flan. Return to the oven for 5 minutes until the bottom is crisp.

- Mix the jam with the raspberries and spoon into the pastry case. Level the top with a palette knife. Brush the rim of the pastry case with egg white.

- Roll out the pastry trimmings and cut into long, thin strips with a sharp knife or pastry cutter. Arrange the strips carefully across the filling to form a lattice pattern.

- Brush the pastry with the remaining beaten egg white and sprinkle over the sugar. Bake in the oven for 25-30 minutes until golden brown.

ORANGE TART

Crostata di Arancia

This is another citrus fruit recipe from Sicily, where oranges are sweet, juicy and plentiful.

SERVES 8

For the filling
1 litre (1¾ pints) freshly-squeezed
   orange juice
grated zest of 4 oranges
8 eggs
350g (12oz) caster sugar
250ml (8fl oz) double cream

crème fraîche, to serve
For the pastry
250g (8oz) plain white or Italian
   type '00' flour
125g (4oz) unsalted butter, chilled
30ml (2 tablespoons) caster sugar
1 free range egg

- Pour the orange juice into a saucepan and boil gently until reduced to 250ml (8fl oz). Leave the juice to cool slightly whilst making the pastry.

- To make the pastry, put the flour into a food processor or large bowl. Dice the butter, add to the flour and blend until the mixture resembles breadcrumbs. Add the sugar and egg and blend until the mixture forms into a ball.

- On a floured surface, roll out the pastry and use to line a 20cm (8 inch) deep-sided, loose-bottomed, fluted flan tin. Chill the tart in the fridge for 30 minutes.

- Pre-heat the oven to 200°C, 400°F, Gas Mark 6.

- Put the tart tin on a baking tray, line with greaseproof paper or foil and weigh down with baking beans. Bake blind in the oven for 15 minutes until the sides of the pastry are crisp. Remove the lining and beans and bake for a further 5 minutes until the bottom is crisp.

- Whisk together the cooled orange juice, orange zest, eggs, sugar and cream until well mixed then pour into the pre-baked pastry case.

- Bake in the oven at 180°C, 350°F, Gas Mark 4 for 35 minutes until softly set.

- Leave to cool before serving with crème fraîche.

STRAWBERRY TART

Crostata di Fragole

This tart is typical of Italy and found in so many pasticceria. Use this recipe to experiment with different fruits when in season – my father loves it with whole black cherries and cherry conserve.

SERVES 6-8

For the pastry
300g (11oz) plain white or Italian type '00' flour
pinch of salt
150g (5oz) unsalted butter, softened
100g (4oz) caster sugar

1 free range egg and 3 egg yolks
grated zest of 1 unwaxed lemon
For the filling
275g (10oz) strawberry high fruit content conserve
450g (1lb) strawberries
icing sugar, for dusting

- To make the pastry, put the flour and salt into a bowl with the butter, sugar, egg and egg yolks and lemon zest. Using your fingertips, knead the ingredients together to form a soft dough. Wrap in greaseproof paper and chill in the fridge for 30 minutes.

- Pre-heat the oven to 190°C, 375°F, Gas Mark 5.

- On a lightly floured surface, roll out three-quarters of the pastry and use to line a 24cm (9½ inch) loose-bottomed flan tin. Spread with the strawberry conserve.

- Roll out the remaining pastry, cut into strips and use to form a lattice on top of the conserve.

- Bake in the oven for 20-25 minutes until golden. Leave to cool in the tin.

- Before serving, decorate with the whole strawberries and dust with sifted icing sugar.

LUCY'S PASTRIES

Sfinci di Lucia

Since my latest baby niece is called Lucy, I shall dedicate this recipe to her. These make a quick and delicious snack, which is crisp on the outside, yet soft in the centre.

MAKES ABOUT 15

2 large free range eggs
75g (3oz) granulated sugar
250g (9oz) ricotta cheese, well drained
15ml (1 tablespoon) vanilla extract
275g (10oz) plain white or Italian type '00' flour

7.5ml (1½ teaspoons) baking powder
2.5ml (½ teaspoon) salt
150ml (¼ pint) milk
olive oil, for deep frying
icing sugar, for dusting

- In a bowl, mix together the eggs, sugar, ricotta cheese and vanilla extract until smooth and creamy. Sift the flour, baking powder and salt together and then add to the egg mixture, blending well until a heavy, sticky batter is formed. Gradually blend in the milk.

- In a deep-fat frying pan, heat the oil until a teaspoon of the batter, when dropped into it, turns crisp. Using 2 tablespoons, drop 2-3 spoonfuls of the batter at a time into the hot oil and fry for 2-3 seconds until crisp and golden brown. Remove with a slotted spoon and drain on kitchen paper.

- Sprinkle with sifted icing sugar and serve at once.

CHERRY AND HAZELNUT TART

Crostata di Ciliege

Cherries are in season in May and June and, as a change from eating them as fresh fruit, this recipe is a good way of using them. (Do use ripe, unblemished cherries.) Hazelnuts give the pastry a rich taste and texture.

SERVES 12

For the pastry
200g (7oz) plain white or Italian
 type '00' flour
pinch of salt
150g (5oz) unsalted butter
100g (4oz) icing sugar
50g (2oz) chopped, toasted
hazelnuts
1 egg yolk
For the topping
700g (1½lb) ripe cherries
350g (12oz) mascarpone cheese
10ml (2 teaspoons) vanilla extract
15ml (1 tablespoon) brandy

- Sift the flour and salt into a bowl and rub in the butter until the mixture resembles fine breadcrumbs. Stir in 75g (3oz) of the sugar and the hazelnuts. Stir in the egg yolk and about 10ml (2 teaspoons) water and mix to form a dough. Wrap in greaseproof paper and chill in the fridge for 30 minutes.

- Meanwhile, stone the cherries.

- Pre-heat the oven to 190°C, 375°F, Gas Mark 5.

- On a lightly floured surface, roll out the pastry and use to line a loose-bottomed 28cm (11 inch) flan tin. Prick the base. Line with greaseproof paper and weigh down with baking beans. Bake in the oven for about 15 minutes until the sides of the pastry are crisp. Remove the lining and beans and return to the oven for 5 minutes until the bottom is crisp.

- In a large bowl, combine the mascarpone cheese with the remaining 25g (1oz) icing sugar, the cherries, vanilla extract and brandy. Spoon into the cooked pastry case and serve.

PIZZA DOLCE

This sweet pizza is made with almond pastry, filled with an exquisite Marsala custard. As it is very rich, only a small serving is necessary. It is especially delicious with a strong espresso.

SERVES 10-12

For the pastry
425g (15oz) ground almonds
200g (7oz) golden caster sugar
90g (3½oz) honey
5ml (1 teaspoon) ground
    cinnamon
grated zest of 1 unwaxed lemon
2 egg whites

For the custard
175g (6oz) golden caster sugar
5 egg yolks
75g (3oz) plain white or Italian
    type '00' flour
500ml (17fl oz) milk
60ml (4 tablespoons) Marsala
100g (4oz) finely chopped
    blanched almonds
icing sugar, for dredging

- Pre-heat the oven to 180°C, 350°F, Gas Mark 4.

- To make the pastry, put the ground almonds, sugar, honey, cinnamon and lemon zest in a bowl and mix together. Add only just enough egg white to make a soft, firm dough (it is important not to add more than you need). Start kneading the mixture together when it is still dry, until it binds together.

- Roll out the pastry to line a 30cm (12 inch) flan tin. Slip the base of the flan tin under the pastry then put in the flan case. (Don't worry if it crumbles a little, just patch it.) Prick the base of the pastry, line with greaseproof paper and weigh down with baking beans.

- Bake it in the oven for 15 minutes until the sides are crisp. Remove the lining and beans and return to the oven for 5 minutes until the bottom is crisp.

- To make the custard, beat together the sugar and egg yolks until light and pale, then beat in the flour. Pour the milk into a heavy-based saucepan and heat until just below boiling point. Gradually pour on to the egg mixture, beating vigorously until well blended. Return to the rinsed pan and bring to the boil, whisking continuously. Simmer for 3 minutes, stirring occasionally so that the custard does not stick to the bottom of the pan. Stir in the Marsala and chopped almonds. Leave to cool.

- When the custard is cool, spread it into the pastry case. Dredge with icing sugar before serving.

PINE KERNEL TART

Torta di Pinoli

This tart is enjoyed throughout Italy and many pasticceria will sell a slice with a coffee for breakfast or to take home. This particular recipe is the very best I know, although there are many regional variations. Please do use fresh pine kernels and store in the fridge to prevent them becoming rancid. There is a huge difference in flavour between Asian and Mediterranean pine kernels – try to find Mediterranean ones if you can, for a better taste.

SERVES 8-12

For the pastry
150g (5oz) unsalted butter, softened
150g (5oz) caster sugar
4 egg yolks
350g (12oz) plain white or Italian type '00' flour
finely grated zest of 1 unwaxed lemon
pinch of salt

For the filling
350g (12oz) ricotta cheese
a few drops of vanilla extract
50ml (2fl oz) double cream
3 egg yolks
100g (4oz) caster sugar
100g (4oz) pine kernels
icing sugar, for dusting

- To make the pastry, put the softened butter, caster sugar and egg yolks in a food processor and mix together. Add the flour, lemon zest and salt and mix again. Wrap in greaseproof paper and chill in the fridge for 1 hour.

- Pre-heat the oven to 170°C, 325°F, Gas Mark 3

- To make the filling, using a wooden spoon, beat the ricotta cheese in a bowl. Add the vanilla extract, double cream, egg yolks, sugar and three-quarters of the pine kernels and mix together.

- On a lightly floured surface, roll out the pastry and use two-thirds to line a 20cm (8 inch) loose-bottomed flan tin. Chill in the fridge for 30 minutes.

- Prick the base with a fork and line with a piece of greaseproof paper and baking beans, then bake in the oven for 20 minutes until golden. Remove the lining and beans. Pour the filling into the pastry case. Roll out the remaining pastry and cut into 1cm (½ inch) strips, the same length as the tart. Use to make a lattice decoration on the tart by laying half the strips at intervals across the surface and the other half across the first layer. Scatter the remaining pine kernels over the top.

- Bake in the oven for 35 minutes until the pastry is crisp and golden and the filling is firm to the touch.

- Leave to cool slightly, then serve warm, dusted with sifted icing sugar.

WALNUT TART

Torta di Noci

The best walnuts come from the Aosta Valley. When possible, do use fresh nuts for their sweetness. In Umbria, where I teach, we grill the walnuts and crack them open especially to make this tart

SERVES 12.

For the pastry
100g (4oz) unsalted butter
50g (2oz) caster sugar
2 large egg yolks
225g (8oz) plain white or Italian type '00' flour
For the filling
75g (3oz) caster sugar

5ml (1 teaspoon) fresh lemon juice
60ml (4 tablespoons) fragrant honey
225g (8oz) unsalted butter
225g (8oz) chopped walnuts
pinch of salt
icing sugar, for dusting
mascarpone cheese, to serve

- To make the pastry, beat together the butter and sugar until light and soft. Add the egg yolks one at a time, then mix in the flour. With your hands, bind the mixture together. Wrap in greaseproof paper and chill in the fridge for 30 minutes.

- Meanwhile, make the filling. Put all the ingredients in a saucepan, bring to the boil and boil for 2 minutes. Remove from the heat and leave to cool.

- Pre-heat the oven to 200°C, 400°F, Gas Mark 6.

- On a lightly floured surface, roll out the pastry and use to line a 22cm (8½ inch) flan tin. Don't worry if the pastry cracks, just press it into the tin and patch if necessary. Trim and re-roll the trimmings for the top. Spread the cooled walnut filling into the case and cover with the pastry top.

- Using the prongs of a fork, seal the edges together and prick the top. Bake in the oven for 30 minutes until golden. Leave to cool in the tin.

- Before serving, dust with sifted icing sugar and serve with a dollop of mascarpone cheese.

LITTLE JAM PASTRIES

Bocconotti

This is another typical recipe from Naples. All the pastry shops sell their own variations of this recipe, some are jam and others are custard-filled. I particularly enjoy these for breakfast.

MAKES 24

For the pastry cream
1 free range egg
15ml (1 tablespoon) caster sugar
15ml (1 tablespoon) plain white or
    Italian type '00' flour
100ml (3½fl oz) single cream
a few drops vanilla extract
grated zest of ½ unwaxed lemon
For the pastry

300g (11oz) plain white or Italian
    type '00' flour
75g (3oz) caster sugar
45ml (3 tablespoons) olive oil
For the filling
about 30ml (2 tablespoons)
    blackberry or strawberry jam
1 egg yolk, beaten
icing sugar, for dusting

- To make the pastry cream, cream together the egg and sugar until pale and thick. Sift in the flour and beat until smooth. Heat the cream in a saucepan until almost boiling, then pour on to the egg mixture, stirring all the time. Return to the pan and cook over a low heat, stirring, until it boils and thickens. Remove the pan from the heat and stir in the vanilla extract and lemon zest. Cover the surface with a piece of greaseproof paper and leave to cool completely.

- Pre-heat the oven to 200°C, 400°F, Gas Mark 6.

- To make the pastry, mix together the flour and sugar. Mix in the oil and 90ml (6 tablespoons) water to make a soft dough. On a floured work surface, roll out the pastry and cut into 7cm (3 inch) circles.

- Place a dab of jam and pastry cream in the centre of each circle. Fold the circle in half and press the edges firmly together to seal. Lay the pastries on a baking tray and brush with the egg yolk.

- Bake in the oven for 12-15 minutes until golden brown. Leave to cool, then serve dusted with sifted icing sugar.

SICILIAN FILLED PASTRIES

Cannoli

These pastries are traditionally made with wooden cannoli tubes, which can be bought from specialist kitchen shops. Should these be difficult to find, I have adapted the recipe so that you can make them without the tubes. Alternatively, you can buy ready made cannoli cases from Italian delicatessens.

MAKES 8

25g (1oz) unsalted butter
1 egg white
50g (2oz) caster sugar
25g (1oz) plain white or Italian type '00' flour
5ml (1 teaspoon) cocoa powder
For the filling
75g (3oz) ricotta cheese
15ml (1 tablespoon) caster sugar

25g (1oz) dark chocolate with 50 per cent cocoa solids
25g (1oz) shelled, peeled and chopped pistachio nuts
grated zest of ½ a lemon
2.5ml (½ teaspoon) vanilla extract
pinch of ground cinnamon
icing sugar and cocoa powder, for dusting

- Pre-heat the oven to 190°C, 375°F, Gas Mark 5. Grease the handles of 2 wooden spoons and line 2 baking trays with baking parchment.

- Melt the butter and leave to cool. Whisk the egg white until stiff, then fold in the sugar. Sift the flour and cocoa powder over the egg mixture and fold in. Trickle the butter around the sides of the bowl and fold in.

- Put tablespoons of the mixture on to the prepared baking trays and spread to circles about 10cm (4 inch) in diameter. Only make 2 per baking tray.

- Bake in the oven for about 7 minutes until firm to the touch.

- Remove from the oven and slide a palette knife under each circle, then wrap around the wooden spoons. Leave to cool for 2-3 minutes, then ease off the handles and cool on a wire rack. Use the remaining mixture in the same way to make 8 pastry tubes.

- To make the filling, put the ricotta cheese into a small bowl and mix in the sugar. Grate the chocolate and fold into the mixture with the nuts, lemon zest, vanilla extract and cinnamon.

- Fill a piping bag with a large, plain nozzle with the ricotta mixture and use to stuff the pastry tubes.

- Place the pastries on a serving dish and dust with sifted icing sugar and cocoa powder. Serve at once.

Ice Creams, Ices and Frozen Desserts

Ice Cream is synonymous with Italy. Everybody visiting Italy returns with great stories of the best-ever ice cream they have enjoyed. My particular favourite in this chapter is Coffee and Cinnamon Ice Cream. Children will adore my recipe for Chocolate Ice Cream. In Italy, ice cream is enjoyed in the evenings, strolling in the piazza – passing the time of day and watching the world go by. It is never sickly, but cool, rich and delicious. Water ices are equally popular, mainly in the south where it is hotter. Lemon Water Ice is especially refreshing.

ITALIAN VANILLA ICE CREAM

Gelato alla Vaniglia

This really is an original recipe for Italian ice cream. It is soft in texture and low in fat because it doesn't contain cream.

SERVES 4-6

700ml (24fl oz) milk	8 large egg yolks
1 vanilla pod	175g (6oz) granulated sugar

- Pour the milk into a medium saucepan and heat gently until warm. Remove from the heat. Split the vanilla pod lengthways and leave to infuse in the warm milk for 20 minutes.

- Using an electric whisk, beat together the egg yolks and sugar until very thick.

- Remove the vanilla pod from the milk, scrape out the seeds. Gradually add the milk to the mixture, then add the vanilla seeds.

- Pour into an ice cream machine and freeze according to the manufacturer's instructions.

- Alternatively, pour into a shallow freezer container and freeze, uncovered, for 1-2 hours until mushy. Turn the mixture into a bowl and, using a fork, break up the ice crystals. Return to the freezer and repeat, breaking up the ice crystals every 30 minutes for 2 hours.

- Return to the freezer to become firm. The texture will be softer than you might expect, but this is correct. Cover the container with a lid for storing

COFFEE AND CINNAMON ICE CREAM

Spumone al Caffè
(See colour photograph)

This is a Neapolitan ice cream, made with cream, custard, and ground coffee. The ground coffee in it may sound unusual but you will be surprised at the result, which is semi-soft and really delicious – I promise.

SERVES 6

4 large egg yolks
100g (4oz) caster sugar
2.5ml (½ teaspoon) freshly ground cinnamon

45ml (3 tablespoons) coarsely ground continental coffee
750ml (1¼ pints) double cream

- Put the egg yolks, sugar, cinnamon and coffee in a heatproof bowl and beat well together.

- Place the bowl over a saucepan of simmering water and, using an electric whisk, whisk the mixture until it has doubled in volume. Remove the bowl from the heat and continue whisking until cool.

- Whip the cream until it just holds its shape, then fold into the egg mixture.

- Pour the mixture into an ice cream machine and freeze according to the manufacturer's instructions.

- Alternatively, pour the mixture into a shallow freezer container and freeze uncovered, for about 1 hour until mushy. Turn the mixture into a chilled bowl and whisk until smooth. Return to the container, freeze again until mushy then whisk again.

- Return to the freezer to become firm. Cover the container with a lid for storing.

CHOCOLATE ICE CREAM

Gelato al Cioccolato

This chapter would not be complete without a recipe for chocolate ice cream. It is for chocolate lovers everywhere. My friend Claudio does not freeze the mixture but serves it as a delicious mousse.

SERVES 4

225g (8oz) dark chocolate with 50 per cent cocoa solids
45ml (3 tablespoons) milk
6 free range eggs, separated

60ml (4 tablespoons) brandy (optional)
300ml (½ pint) whipping cream

- Break the chocolate into a bowl and add the milk. Stand the bowl over a saucepan of simmering water and heat until melted. Remove the bowl from the heat.

- Beat the egg yolks into the mixture, one at a time, then add the brandy, if using. Leave to cool.

- Whip the cream until it holds its shape, then fold into the chocolate mixture. Whisk the egg whites until stiff, then fold into the mixture.

- Pour the mixture into a shallow freezer container and freeze, uncovered, for 2-3 hours until firm.

- Cover the container with a lid for storing.

LEMON ICE CREAM

Gelato al Limone

My love of lemons is well known to everyone who knows me, so it's no surprise that this recipe is one of my favourite ice creams. I hope you enjoy it too.

SERVES 4

thickly pared zest and juice of 3 lemons	100g (4oz) caster sugar 225ml (8fl oz) double cream

- Place the pared lemon zest, 225ml (8fl oz) water and the sugar in a saucepan and bring to the boil. Boil for 2 minutes, then remove from the heat and leave to cool. Strain the syrup into a bowl and finely chop the zest.

- When cold, add the chopped zest, lemon juice and cream to the syrup.

- Pour into an ice cream machine and freeze according to the manufacturer's instructions.

- Alternatively, pour into a shallow freezer container and freeze, uncovered, for 1-2 hours until mushy. Turn the mixture into a bowl and, using a fork, break up the ice crystals. Return to the freezer and repeat, breaking up the ice crystals every 30 minutes for 2 hours.

- Return to the freezer to become firm. Cover the container with a lid for storing.

- Transfer to the fridge 45 minutes before serving.

Fig Ice Cream

Gelato ai Fichi

This recipe uses dried figs, which give the ice cream a more intense flavour.

Serves 4

500g (1lb) dried figs, trimmed	250ml (8fl oz) milk
125g (4oz) granulated sugar	125ml (4fl oz) double cream

- Put the figs and sugar in a food processor and blend until smooth and creamy. Add 125ml (4fl oz) water, the milk and cream and continue blending until well mixed.

- Pour into an ice cream machine and freeze according to the manufacturer's instructions.

- Alternatively, pour into a shallow freezer container and freeze, uncovered, for 1-2 hours until mushy. Turn the mixture into a bowl and, using a fork, break up the ice crystals. Return to the freezer and repeat, breaking up the ice crystals every 30 minutes for 2 hours.

- Return to the freezer to become firm. Cover the container with a lid for storing.

ORANGE WATER ICE

Granita di Arancia

There are so many delicious, refreshing water ices in Italy. In my book,
Real Fast Vegetarian Food, *I have one made with coffee. A granita is
a water ice which is frozen to a granular texture. It is an exquisite,
very cold dessert and perfectly cooling on a hot day.*

SERVES 4

450ml (¾ pint) freshly squeezed orange juice (about 10 oranges)	juice of 1 unwaxed lemon 45ml (3 tablespoons) sugar

- Put all the ingredients in a saucepan and heat gently until the sugar has dissolved, then boil gently for 10 minutes. Leave until cold.

- When cold, pour into an ice cream machine and freeze according to the manufacturer's instructions.

- Alternatively, pour into a shallow freezer container, cover and freeze for about 30 minutes until crystals start to form. Turn the mixture into a bowl and, using a fork, break up the ice crystals. Return to the freezer for a further 30 minutes until firm.

- To serve, spoon into individual glasses.

LEMON WATER ICE

Granita di Limone

This cool, refreshing Italian classic is enjoyed throughout Italy during the blistering hot days of high summer. A variation of this recipe is Raspberry and Lemon water ice with the simple addition of 225g (8oz) raspberries. Purée these and add to the cold syrup.

SERVES 6

175g (6oz) granulated sugar
8 large unwaxed lemons

lemon slices, for decorating (optional)

- Make a sugar syrup by putting the sugar in a saucepan with 450ml (¾ pint) water and heating gently until it dissolves. Bring to the boil then boil gently for 10 minutes without stirring.

- Meanwhile, using a potato peeler, peel the zest from the lemons and add to the sugar syrup. Leave until cold.

- Squeeze 450ml (¾ pint) juice from the lemons and pour into a mixing jug. Strain the cold syrup, stir in the lemon juice and mix well together.

- Pour into an ice cream machine and freeze according to the manufacturer's instructions.

- Alternatively, pour into a shallow freezer container, cover and freeze for about 30 minutes until mushy in texture.

- Remove from the freezer and turn the frozen mixture into a bowl. Beat well with a fork to break down the ice crystals. Return to the freezer for a further 30 minutes until firm.

- To serve, spoon into individual glasses and decorate with lemon slices, if wished.

COFFEE WATER ICE

Granita di Caffè

This is a classical Italian water ice that is ideal to make when you have some unused espresso coffee.

SERVES 4

75g (3oz) sugar, plus 10ml (2 teaspoons)
450ml (¾ pint) strong espresso

coffee
225ml (8fl oz) double cream

- Add the 75g (3oz) of the sugar to the coffee and stir until dissolved. Leave to cool.

- Pour into an ice cream machine and freeze according to the manufacturer's instructions.

- Alternatively, pour the mixture into a shallow freezer container, cover and freeze for about 30 minutes until just beginning to set.

strawberry and pistachio cake
torta di fragole al pistacchio

Chocolate cake
Torta di cioccolato

Cream and Marsala trifle
Zuppa Inglese

Coffee and cinnamon ice cream
Spumone al caffè

Almond and cherry cookie
Biscotti di mandorle e ciglieg

Chocolate truffles
Tartufe al cioccolato

Apricot and almond
Torta di albicocche e man⋯

- Stir with a fork, stirring in the edges. Transfer to a food processor and blend quickly to break up the coffee ice. Alternatively, turn the mixture into a bowl and beat well with a fork.

- Return the mixture to the container and freeze for 30 minutes until firm.

- Whip the cream with the 10ml (2 teaspoons) sugar until stiff.

- To serve, spoon the coffee ice into individual glasses and top with the cream.

APRICOT AND LEMON SORBET

Sorbetto di Albicocca e Limone

The combination of these two luscious fruits is memorable. This recipe is for my mother, a great apricot lover. Be sure to choose apricots that are ripe.

SERVES 6

450g (1lb) ripe apricots	lemons
grated zest and juice of 2 unwaxed	125g (4oz) caster sugar

- Wash the apricots, halve and remove the stones but do not peel.

- Put the apricots, lemon zest and juice and sugar in a food processor and blend until smooth.

- Pour into an ice cream machine and freeze according to the manufacturer's instructions.

- Alternatively, pour into a shallow freezer container and freeze, uncovered, for 1-2 hours until crystals start to form. Turn the mixture into a bowl and, using a fork, break up the ice crystals. Return to the freezer and repeat, breaking up the ice crystals every 30 minutes for 2 hours.

- Return to the freezer to become firm. Cover the container with a lid for storing. Transfer to the fridge 45 minutes before serving in tall glasses.

CASSATA SICILIANA

This is a simple, classic dessert, made from ricotta cheese and sponge cake and should not be confused with Cassata Gelata *which is an ice cream bombe. Do prepare it a day ahead of time.*

SERVES 8-10

500g (1lb) ricotta cheese
250g (8oz) caster sugar
200g (8oz) dark chocolate with 70 per cent cocoa solids
2.5ml (½ teaspoon) freshly ground cinnamon
30ml (2 tablespoons) Amaretto (almond liqueur)
175g (6oz) chopped pistachio nuts

200g (7oz) chopped glacé fruits
1 quantity of Lady's Fingers (see page 184)
½ an Italian Sponge Cake (see page 129), cut horizontally
For the topping
250ml (8fl oz) double cream
15ml (1 tablespoon) Amaretto
glacé fruit, to decorate

- Line the base and sides of a 1.7 litre (3 pint) pudding basin with cling film.

- Beat together the ricotta cheese and sugar until light and fluffy. Divide the mixture in half.

- Chop half of the chocolate into small pieces. Add to one half of the mixture with the cinnamon and Amaretto. Fold the pistachio nuts and fruit through the other half. Cover both mixtures and set aside.

- Use the Ladies Fingers to line the prepared bowl, pressing them firmly around the bowl so that they are even.

- Fill with the fruit ricotta mixture and then the chocolate ricotta mixture. Cover the top with the cake.

- Cover the bowl and freeze for 2 hours or longer.

- Melt the remaining chocolate and pour over the base of the cassata. Return to the freezer for about 15 minutes until set.

- To make the topping, whip the cream and Amaretto together until it just holds its shape.

- Just before serving, turn out the cassata, spread over the cream mixture to completely cover and decorate with glacé fruit.

BISCUIT TORTONI

Bisquit Tortoni

Biscuit Tortoni is a creation of a Neapolitan ice cream maker, Mr. Tortoni. Mr Tortino expanded his career to Paris where he opened the famous Café Napolitaine. This talented creator is popular throughout Italy, especially in Rome.

SERVES 10

300ml (½ pint) double cream
30ml (2 tablespoons) icing sugar
225g (8oz) toasted chopped almonds
30ml (2 tablespoons) rum

225g (8oz) Amaretti biscuits (almond macaroons)
10 glacé or maraschino cherries or Cherries Preserved in Rum (see page 199)

- Arrange 10 paper cake cases on a baking tray.

- Whisk together the cream and icing sugar until stiff. Fold in the almonds. Blend the rum well into the mixture.

- Crumble the Amaretti biscuits into quarters and put pieces in the bottom of the paper cases. Add the cream mixture and top each with a cherry.

- Place in the freezer for 1-2 hours until firm. Store in the freezer for up to 2 weeks.

ICED ZABAGLIONE
Zabaglione Semifreddo

*I just couldn't leave this spectacular pudding out of my book. The
recipe is one of the simplest to make and one that you will never tire of.*

SERVES 4-6

4 egg yolks	150ml (¼ pint) dry Marsala
100g (4oz) caster sugar	150ml (¼ pint) whipping cream

- Put the egg yolks and sugar into a large, heatproof bowl and whisk until the mixture is very pale and leaves a trail when the beaters are lifted.

- Whisk in the Marsala. Stand the bowl over a saucepan of simmering water and continue whisking until the mixture has at least doubled in volume.

- Remove from the heat, stand the bowl in cold water and whisk until the mixture is cool.

- Whip the cream until it just holds its shape. Add to the egg mixture and whisk together.

- Pour the mixture into a freezer container and freeze for about 1½ hours until firm.

- Serve in small-stemmed glasses.

Cakes for Family and Friends

Simple, straightforward and effortless cakes have been included in this chapter. These are everyday cakes gathered from all my family and friends throughout the whole of Italy. I've even asked local restaurants and pastry shops for their special cake recipes that I've enjoyed. Now I would like to pass them on to you, to enjoy with your family and friends.

BLACKBERRY AND CINNAMON CAKE

Torta alle More Aromatizzata alla Cannella

This is crumbly and succulent with blackberries, but you can use other berries as an alternative. This cake is filled with childhood memories for me. It is particularly good served with mascarpone cheese and strong black coffee.

SERVES 8-12

150g (5oz) unsalted butter, softened
150g (5oz) caster sugar
150g (5oz) ground almonds
150g (5oz) self-raising flour
1 free range egg

10ml (2 teaspoons) freshly ground cinnamon
10ml (2 teaspoons) vanilla extract
225g (8oz) fresh blackberries
icing sugar, for dusting

- Pre-heat the oven to 180°C, 350°F, Gas Mark 4. Grease and line the base of a 23cm (9 inch) springform tin.

- Put the butter, sugar, almonds, flour, egg, 5ml (1 teaspoon) of the cinnamon and the vanilla extract in a bowl and beat well together.

- Spread half the mixture into the prepared tin and, using a fork, flatten lightly. Sprinkle over the blackberries and dot over the remaining almond mixture so that it covers the fruit.

- Put the tin on a baking tray and bake in the oven for 1 hour until golden on top but springy. Leave to cool in the tin.

- Dust the top with the remaining sifted cinnamon and icing sugar before serving.

ALMOND CRUMBLE CAKE

Torta Sbrisulona

This is a very old recipe from Northern Italy and, although the result is not dissimilar to shortbread, in Italy it is considered a cake to be served on feast days.

SERVES 10-12

300g (11oz) plain white, or Italian type '00' flour
100g (4oz) medium cornmeal
225g (8oz) unsalted butter
200g (7oz) chopped blanched almonds

200g (7oz) caster sugar
2 egg yolks
finely grated zest of 1 unwaxed lemon
a few drops of vanilla extract

- Pre-heat the oven to 170°C, 325°F, Gas Mark 3. Grease a 23cm (9 inch) round cake tin.

- Put the flour and cornmeal in a bowl, then rub in the butter until the mixture resembles breadcrumbs.

- Stir in the almonds and sugar, then add the egg yolks, lemon zest and vanilla extract. Knead to form a smooth, stiff dough.

- Put the mixture into the prepared tin and smooth the surface. Bake in the oven for about 45 minutes until firm to the touch. Turn out onto a wire rack and leave to cool.

ORANGE AND LEMON CAKE

Torta Limone e Arancia

A wonderful moist, aromatic cake. It can be made in the same way with clementines, when they are in season.

SERVES 8-10

4 medium oranges	225g (8oz) ground almonds
1 unwaxed lemon	icing sugar, for dusting
175g (6oz) caster sugar	mascarpone cheese, to serve
6 free range eggs, separated	

- Put the whole oranges and lemon in a heavy-based saucepan and cover with cold water. Bring to the boil and simmer for 2 hours, topping up with water if necessary. Drain and leave to cool.

- Pre-heat the oven to 170°C, 325°F, Gas Mark 3. Grease and line a 23cm (9 inch) round cake tin.

- Cut the fruits in half and discard any pips. Put the fruit, in batches, in a food processor or liquidiser and blend with the sugar to form a purée.

- Put the purée in a large bowl and, using a hand mixer, beat in the egg yolks and almonds.

- Whisk the egg whites until stiff but not too dry, then fold into the fruit mixture.

- Gently spoon the mixture into the prepared tin and carefully level the surface. Bake in the oven for 1½ hours until golden, firm to the touch, and a skewer, when inserted in the centre, comes out clean. Leave to cool in the tin.

- Dust with sifted icing sugar before serving with mascarpone cheese.

HARVEST GRAPE CAKE

Torta Vendemmia

I first enjoyed this cake during a long weekend trip to see friends in Verona. It should be made when black grapes are at their best after the harvest at the end of September or early October.

SERVES 8

450g (1lb) seedless sweet black grapes
225g (8oz) plain white or Italian type '00' flour
150g (5oz) golden caster sugar
7.5ml (1½ teaspoons) baking powder
5 free range eggs
45ml (3 tablespoons) olive oil
icing sugar, for dusting (optional)

- Pre-heat the oven to 180°C, 350°F, Gas Mark 4. Grease a deep, round 20cm (8 inch) cake tin.

- Dust the grapes with a little flour. Put the flour, sugar and baking powder in a large bowl. Add the eggs, one at a time, beating well after each addition, until the mixture is the consistency of batter. Add the grapes and olive oil and mix well together.

- Pour the mixture into the prepared tin and bake for 45 minutes until golden and well risen. Turn out onto a wire rack and leave to cool.

- When cold, dust the top with sifted icing sugar, if liked.

LEMON POLENTA CAKE

Polentina al Limone

There are many variations of this cake – I do hope you will like mine. I like to serve it with a spoonful of mascarpone cheese and coffee.

SERVES 8-12

275g (10oz) unsalted butter
225g (8oz) caster sugar
6 free range eggs, separated
175g (6oz) ground almonds

100g (4oz) coarse polenta
grated zest and juice of 4 unwaxed
   lemons
icing sugar, for dusting

- Pre-heat the oven to 180°C, 350°F, Gas Mark 4. Grease and line a 25cm (10 inch) round, loose-bottomed cake tin.

- Cream the butter and sugar together until thick and creamy. Add the egg yolks, one at a time, beating between each addition.

- Add the almonds, polenta, lemon zest and juice to the mixture and mix well together.

- Whisk the egg whites until stiff. Using a metal spoon, fold into the mixture.

- Pour the mixture into the prepared tin and bake in the oven for about 50 minutes, until golden and firm to the touch.

- Leave to cool in the tin. When cold, remove from the tin and dust with sifted icing sugar.

WARM PLUM AND HAZELNUT CAKE

Torta alle Susine e Nocciole

The plums give this cake a good moist texture. It is best eaten warm with mascarpone cheese.

SERVES 4

450g (1 lb) plums
100g (4oz) unsalted butter
75g (3oz) soft brown sugar
2 free range eggs

225g (8oz) self-raising flour
50g (2oz) chopped hazelnuts
icing sugar, to decorate

- Pre-heat the oven to 190°C, 375°F, Gas mark 5. Grease and line a 20cm (8 inch) round cake tin.

- Cut the plums into quarters, discarding the stones.

- Cream together the butter and sugar until light and fluffy, then beat in the eggs, one at a time. Fold in the flour. Carefully fold in the plums, then pile the mixture into the prepared tin.

- Sprinkle the hazelnuts over the top and bake in the oven for **45-50** minutes or until golden brown and firm to the touch. Leave to cool slightly in the tin.

- Turn out and serve slightly warm, dusted with sifted icing sugar.

ROSIE'S CAKE

Torta di Rosina

Rosie is a firm friend of mine, who was brought up in a small Italian community in Africa. We love talking about food and Rosie recently made this truly wonderful cake for me. I just couldn't stop eating it.

SERVES 8-10

4 Cox's orange pippin apples
150ml (¼ pint) sweet red wine
3 large free range eggs
100g (4oz) caster sugar
150ml (¼ pint) sunflower oil
15ml (1 tablespoon) vanilla extract

200g (8oz) self-raising flour
30ml (2 tablespoons) ground
cinnamon
For the topping
50g (2oz) whole blanched almonds
50g (2oz) caster sugar

- Grease and line a deep 25cm (10 inch) loose-bottomed cake tin. Peel and slice the apples, put in a bowl, pour over the wine and leave for 20 minutes.

- Preheat the oven to 180°C, 350°F, Gas Mark 4.

- Whisk together the eggs and sugar until thick and creamy. Gradually whisk in the oil and vanilla extract. Fold in the flour, 1 tablespoon at a time and, finally, add the apple and wine mixture and 15ml (1 tablespoon) of the cinnamon. Stir gently until well mixed. Pour into the prepared tin and bake in the oven for 1 hour until firm to the touch.

- Meanwhile, prepare the topping. Roughly chop the almonds and mix together with the sugar and remaining cinnamon. Sprinkle over the top of the cake as soon as it is cooked. Remove from the tin and leave to cool.

ITALIAN SPONGE CAKE

Pan di Spagna

It is curious to find a Spanish cake so popular in Italy. This cake came to Italy via Sicily; the Spanish were invaders of this fabled island. This is a cake which is also good for using in trifles.

SERVES 12

5 large free range eggs, separated	grated zest of 2 unwaxed lemons
225g (8oz) caster sugar	5ml (1 teaspoon) vanilla extract
200g (7oz) plain white or Italian type '00' flour	5ml (1 teaspoon) rum

- Pre-heat the oven to 180°C, 350°F, Gas Mark 4. Grease and flour a 23cm (9 inch) round cake tin.

- Whisk together the egg yolks and sugar until thick and creamy. Sift the flour.

- Whisk the egg whites until stiff, then gently fold into the egg mixture. Gradually fold in the flour. Add the lemon zest, vanilla and rum and mix together until well blended.

- Pour into the prepared tin and bake in the oven for 30-35 minutes until golden brown and well risen. Turn out onto a wire rack and leave to cool.

ALMOND ORANGE CAKE

Torta di Mandorle con Arancia

This cake is light, moist and full of flavour. We use a lot of almonds in Italy as they grow so prolifically. The recipe comes from an aunt of mine in Naples.

SERVES 8

4 large free range eggs, separated
225g (8oz) granulated sugar
60ml (4 tablespoons) potato flour
350g (12oz) ground almonds

grated zest of 3 oranges and juice of 2 oranges
icing sugar, for dusting

- Pre-heat the oven to 180°C, 350°F, Gas Mark 4. Grease and flour a 20cm (8 inch) springform cake tin.

- Beat together the egg yolks and sugar until pale, thick and creamy. Fold in the potato flour, then fold in the almonds, orange zest and juice.

- Whisk the egg whites until stiff, then fold into the mixture. Turn into the prepared tin.

- Bake in the oven for 45 minutes until golden brown and firm to the touch. Remove from the tin and leave to cool on a wire rack.

- Dust with sifted icing sugar before serving.

CARROT CAKE

Torta di Carote

This recipe has been given to me by Antonietta Balducci, a great friend of mine from Umbria. She has just opened her own pasticceria in the village of Selci Larma. It is a moist cake that is best eaten on the day it is made.

SERVES 12

300g (11oz) carrots
5 free range eggs, separated
200g (7oz) caster sugar
250g (9oz) ground hazelnuts
10ml (2 teaspoons) vanilla extract
75g (3oz) fresh breadcrumbs
2.5ml (½ teaspoon) baking powder

grated zest of 1 lemon
15ml (1 tablespoon) rum
2.5ml (½ teaspoon) ground
   cinnamon
pinch of salt
icing sugar, for dusting

- Pre-heat the oven to 170°C, 325°F, Gas Mark 3. Grease and line a 25cm (10 inch) round cake tin.

- Peel and grate the carrots.

- Put the egg yolks and sugar in a heatproof bowl, standing over a saucepan of gently simmering water. Whisk for 10-15 minutes until the mixture is thick and creamy.

- Remove from the heat and fold in the grated carrots, hazelnuts, vanilla extract, breadcrumbs, baking powder, lemon zest, rum, cinnamon and salt.

- Whisk the egg whites until stiff, then carefully fold into the mixture.

- Pour the mixture into the prepared tin and bake for 1 hour until firm to the touch. Turn out onto a wire rack and leave to cool.

- Dust with sifted icing sugar before serving.

CHOCOLATE CAK

Torta di Cioccolato
(See colour photograph)

This is one of my all-time favourite recipes and since I've been making it for so long, I've tended to experiment with it a lot. It was traditionally made at Christmas time but it is now made and enjoyed all year round. To enjoy the cake at its best, eat with a dollop of mascarpone and strong black coffee. It can be kept for a week, but I doubt that you will be able to resist it for so long.

SERVES 10-12

225g (8oz) dark chocolate with 70 per cent cocoa solids
100g (4oz) unsalted butter
5 free range eggs, separated

150g (5oz) caster sugar
50ml (2fl oz) brandy
90g (3½oz) fine polenta
icing sugar, for dusting

- Pre-heat the oven to 180°C, 350°F, Gas Mark 4. Grease and flour a 25cm (10 inch) loose-bottomed, round cake tin.

- Break the chocolate into a small saucepan, add the butter and heat gently until melted. Remove from the heat.

- Whisk together the egg yolks and sugar until thick and creamy. Fold in the chocolate mixture, rum or brandy and polenta and mix together well.

- Whisk the egg whites until stiff but not too dry and fold into the chocolate mixture.

- Pour into the prepared tin and bake in the oven for 30-40 minutes until firm to the touch but still slightly moist. Leave to cool in the tin. The cake will rise, then sink and crack on top, but don't be alarmed.

- When cold, dust with sifted icing sugar.

CHOCOLATE AND CHESTNUT CAKE

Torta di Castagne e Cioccolata

This is a rich cake which I like to serve with Italian vanilla ice cream.
You will find the recipe for this on page 103.

SERVES 6

25g (1oz) plain white or Italian type '00' flour, plus extra for dusting

225g (8oz) chocolate with 70 per cent cocoa solids

100g (4oz) unsalted butter

4 large free range eggs, separated

300g (11oz) canned, sweetened chestnut purée

5ml (1 teaspoon) vanilla extract

1.25ml (¼ teaspoon) cream of tartar

50g (2oz) caster sugar

icing sugar, for dusting

- Pre-heat the oven to 180°C, 350°F, Gas Mark 4. Grease and line a 20cm (8 inch) deep round cake tin. Dust with flour.

- Break the chocolate into a bowl and add the butter. Place over a saucepan of simmering water and heat, stirring constantly, until smooth. Take care not to overheat. Remove from the heat.

- Sift the flour into a bowl, add the egg yolks, chestnut purée and vanilla extract and whisk together. Stir in the chocolate mixture.

- Whisk together the egg whites and cream of tartar until they just hold their shape, then gradually whisk in the sugar until stiff. Do not overbeat.

- Fold a quarter of the egg whites into the chocolate mixture, then the remaining whites.

- Pour into the prepared tin and bake in the oven for 40-45 minutes, until a skewer, inserted into the centre, comes out moist but not sticky. Leave the cake to cool in the tin. It will have risen and then dropped slightly in the centre.

- When cold, turn out and dust with sifted icing sugar before serving.

HAZELNUT AND CHOCOLATE CAKE

Torta al Cioccolato e Nocciola

I am permanently in pursuit of the perfect chocolate cake and I am always trying new recipes. This particular cake is dense and dotted with hazelnuts. For extra indulgence, add 2 tablespoons of rum with the cocoa powder.

SERVES 8-10

175g (6oz) unsalted butter
125g (4oz) caster sugar
5 free range eggs
15ml (1 tablespoon) vanilla extract
125g (4oz) plain white or Italian type '00' flour

2.5 ml (½ teaspoon) salt
50g (2oz) cocoa powder
5ml (1 teaspoon) baking powder
175g (6oz) toasted chopped hazelnuts
45ml (3 tablespoons) icing sugar

- Pre-heat the oven to 180°C, 350°F, Gas Mark 4. Grease and line a 23cm (9 inch) loose-bottomed cake tin.

- In a large bowl and using an electric mixer, cream together the butter and sugar until pale and fluffy. Add 1 egg and the vanilla extract and whisk in well.

- Sift together the flour, salt, cocoa and baking powder. Using a metal spoon, fold in 30ml (2 tablespoons) of the flour mixture to the egg mixture. Continue to add the eggs alternately with the flour mixture until all the ingredients have been incorporated. Fold in the nuts.

- Pour the mixture into the prepared tin and bake in the oven for 40-50 minutes until firm to the touch and the cake is coming away from the sides of the tin. Leave to cool in the tin.

- Before serving, dust the cake with sifted icing sugar.

FRUIT CAKE RING

Ciambella di Frutta

I have enjoyed this in Bar Sandi in Perugia where I take my students for coffee and cake. I've always arrived when it's been too busy to ask for the recipe, so this is my own version.

SERVES 8

75g (3oz) dried figs
75g (3oz) dried apricots
225g (8oz) unsalted butter
200g (7oz) caster sugar
4 free range eggs, separated
225g (8oz) plain white or Italian
type '00' flour
15ml (1 tablespoon) ground
   cinnamon
50g (2oz) raisins
grated zest of 1 lemon
icing sugar, for dusting

- Pre-heat the oven to 200°C, 400°F, Gas Mark 6. Grease and flour a 20cm (8 inch) savarin mould.

- Chop the figs and apricots into small pieces.

- Put the butter and sugar in a bowl and cream together until pale and fluffy. Add the egg yolks and mix well together. Sift the flour and cinnamon and fold into the creamed mixture.

- Add the figs, apricots, raisins and lemon zest and mix well to blend.

- Whisk the egg whites until stiff. Then, using a metal spoon, fold into the creamed mixture.

- Spoon into the prepared tin and bake in the oven for 30 minutes, until a skewer inserted into the centre comes out clean. Turn out on to a wire rack and leave to cool.

- When cold, dust with sifted icing sugar.

GENOESE SPONGE

Torta Genovese

This light sponge is ideal to use as the base for all Italian gâteaux. It can be simply filled with cream or another filling of your choice.

SERVES 8-12

50g (2oz) unsalted butter
4 free range eggs
100g (4oz) caster sugar

pinch of salt
100g (4oz) plain white or Italian type '00' flour

- Pre-heat the oven to 180°C, 350°F, Gas Mark 4. Grease and line a 23cm (9in) round cake tin.

- Melt the butter, then set aside to cool.

- Put the eggs, sugar and salt in a heatproof bowl, standing over a saucepan of gently simmering water. Whisk until the mixture is thick, pale and tripled in volume.

- Remove the bowl from the heat and continue to whisk until the mixture is cool.

- Sift the flour over the top of the mixture. Slowly trickle the cooled, melted butter around the edge of the bowl then, using a metal spoon, gently fold in both ingredients.

- Pour the mixture into the prepared tin and bake in the oven for 25-30 minutes until golden brown, firm to the touch and shrunk slightly from the sides of the tin. Leave to cool in the tin for 1-2 minutes, then turn out onto a wire rack to cool completely.

PLE AND ROSEMARY CAKE

Torta alle Mele e Rosmarino

This is a quite delicious combination. I first enjoyed it in Venice and think the rosemary gives it a very memorable flavour. It is beautifully moist and is best eaten on the day it is made.

SERVES 8-12

100g (4oz) unsalted butter
350g (12oz) Braeburn or Cox's
  orange pippin apples (about 3)
4 free range eggs
150g (5oz) caster sugar
150g (5oz) plain white or Italian
  type '00' flour

5ml (1 teaspoon) baking powder
pinch of salt
5ml (1 teaspoon) finely chopped
  fresh rosemary
finely grated zest of 1 unwaxed
  lemon
icing sugar, for dusting

- Pre-heat the oven to 180°C, 350°F, Gas Mark 4. Grease a 23cm (9 inch) deep round cake tin.

- Melt the butter then set aside to cool. Core, peel and thinly slice the apples.

- Put the eggs and sugar in a heatproof bowl, standing over a saucepan of gently simmering water. Whisk for 10-15 minutes until the mixture is thick, pale and leaves a trail when the beaters are lifted out. Remove the bowl from the heat and continue whisking until the mixture is cool.

- Sift the flour, baking powder and salt together. Gently fold half the flour and the chopped rosemary into the whisked eggs and sugar.

- Slowly trickle the melted butter around the edge of the bowl and gently fold in. (Take care not to stir the mixture too heavily or it will lose its air.)

- Fold in the remaining flour and the lemon zest. Lastly, fold in the apples.

- Pour the cake mixture into the prepared tin. Bake in the oven for about 40 minutes until a skewer, inserted in the centre, comes out clean.

- Leave the cake to rest in the tin for about 5 minutes, then turn out onto a wire rack and leave to cool.

- Just before serving, sift icing sugar over the top of the cake.

ꓮIST CHERRY CAKE

Torta alle Ciliege

This wonderful recipe comes from my good friend in Verona. It is for making when fresh cherries are in season.

SERVES 8

700g (1½lb) fresh cherries	type '00' flour
100g (4oz) unsalted butter	5ml (1 teaspoon) baking powder
150g (5oz) caster sugar	15ml (1 tablespoon) brandy
4 free range eggs, separated	pinch of salt
200g (7oz) plain white or Italian	icing sugar, for dusting

- Pre-heat the oven to 180°C, 350°F, Gas Mark 4. Grease and flour a 20cm (8 inch) round, loose-bottomed cake tin.

- Wash and remove the stones from the cherries.

- Put the butter and sugar in a bowl and cream together until light and fluffy. Beat in the egg yolks, one at a time, with a little of the plain flour. Sift the remaining flour and baking powder together and mix into the creamed mixture with the brandy.

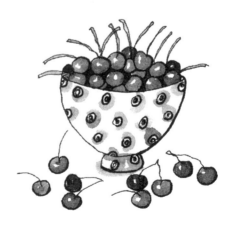

- Whisk the egg whites and salt together until stiff. Using a metal spoon, add 45ml (3 tablespoons) of the whisked egg whites to the creamed mixture and mix well. Mix in the remaining egg whites, then carefully spoon into the prepared tin.

- Scatter the prepared cherries over the top of the cake and press them down lightly into the cake mixture.

- Bake in the oven for 40-50 minutes until the cake is well risen and firm to the touch. Cover the cake with foil after about 40 minutes to prevent it from over-browning. Leave to cool.

- When cold, remove from the tin and dust with sifted icing sugar before serving.

PISTACHIO CAKE

Torta al Pistacchio

Other nuts can be substituted in this sumptuous, yet simple cake from Sicily. Walnuts work well. It is a very rich cake and you can dust with icing sugar instead of topping with cream, if you prefer.

SERVES 10-12

6 eggs, separated
250g (9oz) granulated sugar
30ml (2 tablespoons) plain white or Italian type '00' flour
10ml (2 teaspoons) baking powder
2.5ml (½ teaspoon) salt

350g (12oz) finely chopped pistachio or other nuts
300ml (½ pint) double cream
extra whole pistachio nuts for decorating

- Pre-heat the oven to 180°C, 350°F, Gas mark 4. Grease and line a 23cm (9 inch) deep, round cake tin.

- Beat together the egg yolks and half of the sugar until thick and creamy.

- Sift together the flour, baking powder and salt, then mix into the egg yolk mixture. Gradually beat in the remaining sugar. Fold in the nuts.

- Whisk the egg whites until stiff, then fold into the mixture.

- Pour the mixture into the prepared tin and bake in the oven for about 45 minutes until well risen, golden and firm to the touch. Turn out and cool on a wire rack.

- Before serving, whisk the cream until stiff. Spread on top of the cake and decorate with the whole pistachio nuts.

COUNTRY RICE CAKE

Torta Campagnola

I cannot resist this cake. It always reminds me of my Grandpa, who loved the cake and had a real liking for rice. You would imagine that the rice would make it heavy but, in fact, it is light and fragrant.

SERVES 8-10

150g (5oz) unsalted butter
25g (1oz) toasted, fine
    breadcrumbs
100g (4oz) raisins
30ml (2 tablespoons) Marsala
200ml (7fl oz) milk
100g (4oz) sugar

grated zest of 2 lemons
2.5ml (½ teaspoon) salt
175g (6oz) arborio rice
100g (4oz) candied peel
2 large free range eggs, separated
15ml (1 tablespoon) vanilla extract

- Grease a 1.1 litre (2 pint) ovenproof pudding basin with15g (½oz) of the butter. Coat the basin with the breadcrumbs, shaking out the excess. Put in the fridge until ready to fill.

- In a small bowl, soak the raisins in the Marsala for at least 30 minutes, or preferably overnight.

- In a large saucepan, mix together the milk, 200ml (7fl oz) water, the sugar, lemon zest and salt. Bring the mixture to the boil, add the rice and simmer for 12-15 minutes, stirring occasionally, until all the liquid is absorbed and the mixture is of a soft, dropping consistency. Turn into a bowl and leave to cool slightly.

- Pre-heat the oven to 180°C, 350°F, Gas Mark 4.

- Finely chop the candied peel. Add to the rice with the egg yolks, vanilla extract, remaining butter and the raisins and Marsala and mix together.

- Whisk the egg whites until stiff, then fold into the rice mixture. Spread the rice evenly in the prepared basin.

- Bake in the oven for 40-50 minutes or until a knife inserted in the centre comes out clean. Leave to cool in the basin.

- When cold, invert the cake onto a serving plate. Cut into slim wedges to serve.

SPICED HONEY CAKE

Torta al Miele

I love honey that is rich and fragrant. In Italy we have so many varieties, such as chestnut, rosemary, sunflower, lavender and lemon blossom. This is a moist cake, best eaten the day after it is made.

MAKES 12 SQUARES

225g (8oz) self-raising flour
5ml (1 teaspoon) ground
   cinnamon
2.5ml (½ teaspoon) grated nutmeg
1.25ml (¼ teaspoon) mixed spice

75g (3oz) unsalted butter
100g (4oz) soft brown sugar
175g (6oz) of your favourite honey
2 large free range eggs
about 175ml (6fl oz) milk

- Pre-heat the oven to 170°C, 325°F, Gas Mark 3. Grease and line a 28x23cm (11x9 inch) roasting tin with baking parchment.

- Sift the flour and spices into a large bowl. Put the butter, sugar and honey in a saucepan and heat gently until the ingredients become runny. Remove from the heat and leave to cool.

- Crack the eggs into a measuring jug and make up to 300ml (½ pint) with milk. Using a fork, whisk together.

- Pour the melted mixture into the sifted dry ingredients and add the egg and milk mixture. Using a balloon whisk, blend together the ingredients. Pour the batter into the prepared tin.

- Bake in the oven for about 1 hour until a skewer, inserted in the centre, comes out clean. (Do not touch the surface – it's hot!) Leave to cool in the tin.

ORANGE RING CAKE

Ciambellone al Arancia

This recipe comes from Florence and is very popular with children. It keeps well in an air-tight tin.

SERVES 6-8

150g (5oz) unsalted butter
2 free range eggs, separated
100ml (3½fl oz) milk
200g (7oz) caster sugar
grated zest of 2 oranges

200g (7oz) plain white or Italian type '00' flour
5ml (1 teaspoon) baking powder
icing sugar, for dusting

- Pre-heat the oven to 180°C, 350°F, Gas Mark 4. Grease and flour a 1.7 litre (3 pint) ring mould.

- Melt the butter and set aside to cool. Whisk the egg whites until stiff. Add the egg yolks, milk, sugar and orange zest and beat for 1-2 minutes.

- Sift over the flour and baking powder and, using a metal spoon, fold in alternately with the melted butter.

- Spoon the mixture into the prepared tin and bake in the oven for about 30 minutes until golden and firm to the touch. Leave in the tin for about 5 minutes, then turn out onto a wire rack and leave to cool.

- Before serving, dust with sifted icing sugar.

RUM CAKE

Torta al Rhum

This is a classical Italian cake and this is my favourite variation of it. It is best eaten on the day it is made, accompanied by an espresso coffee.

SERVES 12

200g (7oz) unsalted butter
6 free range eggs
200g (7oz) caster sugar
225g (8oz) plain white or Italian type '00' flour
5ml (1 teaspoon) vanilla extract
60ml (4 tablespoons) dark rum

For the rum butter frosting
100g (4oz) unsalted butter, softened
225g (8oz) icing sugar
1 egg, beaten
5ml (1 teaspoon) vanilla extract
30ml (2 tablespoons) dark rum

- Pre-heat the oven to 180°C, 350°F, Gas Mark 4. Grease and flour a deep, 23cm (9 inch) round cake tin.

- Melt the butter and set aside to cool. Put the eggs and sugar in a heatproof bowl, standing over a saucepan of gently simmering water. Whisk until the mixture is thick, pale and tripled in volume.

- Remove from heat and gradually fold in the flour. Slowly trickle the melted butter around the edge of the bowl, then fold in the vanilla extract.

- Pour the mixture into the prepared tin and bake in the oven for 30-35 minutes until golden brown and firm to the touch. Turn out onto a wire rack and leave to cool.

- When cool, cut the cake in half, sprinkle each layer with rum.

- To make the frosting, cream the butter until it is soft and fluffy. Gradually beat in some of the sugar. Beat in the egg, vanilla extract and rum. Gradually beat in the remaining sugar.

- When the cake has cooled completely, spread the frosting over 1 layer and put the second layer on top. Spread the frosting over the second layer, then over the side of the cake.

- Chill the cake in the fridge to harden the frosting and make it easier for slicing.

Cakes for Special Occasions

Here I've included some really important, classical Italian recipes that have been handed down to me by my relatives. These family recipes include Panettone, Easter Dove and the more unusual Chocolate Aubergine Cake. They really are special and, although they take a little longer to prepare, it's well worth the effort. Amongst the recipes you will find something for Christmas, Easter, family celebrations and other special occasions.

SPICED CHRISTMAS FRUIT CAKE

Pan Speziale

This is the special Christmas cake of Bologna. The recipe was created by the monks of Certosa, who made it especially for the Cardinal Lambertini. It should be made one month in advance.

SERVES 16

250g (9oz) raisins
45ml (3 tablespoons) Marsala
75ml (5 tablespoons) fragrant honey
225g (8oz) caster sugar
75g (3oz) unsalted butter
15ml (1 tablespoon) fennel seeds or aniseed
5ml (1 teaspoon) ground cinnamon
125g (4oz) dark chocolate with 50 per cent cocoa solids

6 eating apples
125g (4oz) candied orange peel
500g (1lb 2oz) plain white or Italian type '00' flour
225g (8oz) coarsely chopped, blanched almonds
125g (4oz) pine kernels
2.5ml (½ teaspoon) baking powder
45ml (3 tablespoons) apricot jam
crystallised fruit and blanched, toasted almonds, to decorate

- Soak the raisins in the Marsala for at least 30 minutes, but preferably overnight.

- Pre-heat the oven to 180°C, 350°F, Gas Mark 4. Grease and line a 23cm (9 inch) deep, round cake tin.

- Heat together the honey, sugar, butter and 30ml (2 tablespoons) water until the sugar dissolves. Crush the fennel seeds or aniseed and add to the mixture with the cinnamon. Pour into a large mixing bowl.

- Coarsely chop the chocolate, peel and grate the apples and chop the orange peel. Add the raisins, chocolate, apples, orange peel, flour, almonds, pine kernels and baking powder and mix well together.

- Pour the mixture into the prepared tin and bake in the oven for about 1 hour 45 minutes, or until a skewer inserted in the centre comes out clean. Leave to cool in the tin for 15 minutes, before turning out onto a wire cooling rack and leaving to cool completely.

- When cold, wrap in parchment paper and then foil and store for 1 month before eating.

- After 1 month, or before Christmas, brush with two-thirds of the jam and stud with the crystallised fruit and almonds. Brush with the remaining jam.

STRAWBERRY AND PISTACHIO CAKE

Torta di Fragole al Pistacchio
(See colour photograph)

This is truly delicious and it will win you many gasps of approval as it looks so stunning. Make it when strawberries are at their best.

SERVES 8-12

50g (2oz) unsalted butter
150g (5oz) blanched pistachio nuts
6 free range eggs, beaten
150g (5oz) caster sugar
a few drops of vanilla extract
150g (5oz) plain white or Italian

type '00' flour
For the filling and decoration
350g (12oz) fresh strawberries plus
  a few to decorate
15ml (1 tablespoon) Marsala
600ml (1 pint) double cream

- Pre-heat the oven to 180°C, 350°F, Gas Mark 4. Grease with butter and line two 20cm (8 inch) round sandwich tins.

- Finely chop the pistachio nuts. Melt the butter in a small pan and leave to cool.

- Put the eggs, sugar and vanilla extract in a bowl. Whisk until pale and thick enough to leave a ribbon-like trail for 8 seconds when the whisk is lifted.

- Sift the flour and fold half into the egg mixture. Pour the cooled butter around the edge of the mixture and carefully fold in the remaining flour. Divide the mixture in half and spoon one half into one of the prepared tins. Fold 25g (1oz) of the pistachio nuts into the remaining mixture and pour into the other tin.

- Bake in the oven for 35-40 minutes or until the cakes have just started shrinking from the side of the tins.

- Cool in the tins for 5 minutes. Turn out on to a wire rack and leave to cool completely.

- To fill and decorate, thinly slice the 350g (12oz) of strawberries. Sprinkle the Marsala over the plain cake, then split both cakes in half horizontally. Whip the cream until it just holds its shape and divide into 2 portions. Set one portion aside.

- Place a pistachio cake layer on a flat plate and spread over half of 1 portion of the cream. Add a plain cake layer, the strawberries, another pistachio cake layer and the remaining cream. Top with the plain cake layer.

- Coat the top and sides of the cake with two-thirds of the reserved portion of cream. Lightly press the remaining pistachio nuts on the sides of the cake. Spoon the remaining cream, in blobs, around the top of the cake and decorate with the remaining strawberries.

CHOCOLATE AND CAKE

Torta al Cioccolata e Rhum

Rich and delicious, this cake is another speciality of Bologna. The people from here have a sheer love of food, as this cake helps to prove.

SERVES 8-10

175g (6oz) dark chocolate with 70 per cent cocoa solids
45ml (3 tablespoons) rum
175g (6oz) unsalted butter
175g (6oz) caster sugar
6 free range eggs, separated
75g (3oz) self raising flour
75g (3oz) ground almonds

For the filling
300ml (½ pint) double cream
30ml (2 tablespoons) icing sugar
For the coating
45ml (3 tablespoons) apricot conserve
450g (1lb) dark chocolate with 70 per cent cocoa solids
icing sugar, for dusting

- Pre-heat the oven to 180°C, 350°F, Gas Mark 4. Grease and line the base and sides of a 23cm (9 inch) deep, round cake tin.

- Break the chocolate into a heatproof bowl and add the rum. Stand the bowl over a saucepan of simmering water and heat until melted. Remove from the heat and leave to cool slightly.

- Put the butter and sugar in a bowl and cream together until light and fluffy, then gradually beat in the egg yolks. Beat in the chocolate. Whisk the eggs until stiff, then fold into the mixture. Using a metal spoon, fold the flour and almonds into the egg mixture.

- Pour the mixture into the prepared tin and bake in the oven for 40-45 minutes until firm to the touch. Leave to cool in the tin, then turn out and carefully slice in half horizontally.

To make the filling, whip the cream with the icing sugar until it just holds its shape. Use the cream to sandwich the cake halves together.

- Melt the apricot conserve then push through a sieve. Brush the conserve all over the cake, then place on a large serving plate.

- To make the chocolate coating, cut a piece of parchment paper 75x6cm (30x2½ inch). Fold under 2.5cm (1 inch) of the paper at each end of the strip to form handles. Break the chocolate into a bowl standing over a pan of simmering water and heat until melted. Using a brush, cover one side of the parchment paper completely with a fairly thick layer of chocolate. Spread the remaining chocolate onto a cold marble slab. Leave the chocolate strip until set but still flexible.

- Before the chocolate on the marble slab sets, using a large knife, push the blade across the surface of the chocolate to roll pieces off in long curls to form caraque. Cover the top of the cake with overlapping curls of chocolate caraque. Dust with icing sugar before serving. Lift the chocolate strip by the handles and place around the side of the cake, pressing so that it sticks to the apricot conserve. Carefully peel away the paper.

CHOCOLATE AND AUBERGINE CAKE

Torta di Melanzane al Cioccolato

This unusual combination of ingredients combines wonderfully. It is made on the Feast Day of the Patron Saint of my family's village. It's not the healthiest of recipes but a once-in-a-while indulgence – you can't always be good!

SERVES 8-10

1 large or two medium aubergines
50g (2oz) plain white or Italian type '00' flour, for dusting
3 free range eggs, beaten
30-60ml (2-4 tablespoons) olive oil
400g (14oz) dark chocolate with
70 per cent cocoa solids
25g (1oz) unsalted butter
60ml (4 tablespoons) Morello cherry conserve or jam
icing sugar (infused with a vanilla pod), for sprinkling

- Grease and line a 20cm (8 inch) loose-bottomed cake tin.

- Thinly slice the aubergine. Sprinkle with salt, put in a bowl, cover and weigh down. Leave for 30 minutes.

- Rinse the aubergine slices and pat dry. Dust in the flour and then dip into the beaten eggs.

- Heat a frying pan and add the oil. When the oil is hot, add the aubergine slices, about 6 slices at a time, and fry for 2-3 minutes, turning once, until golden. Drain on kitchen paper.

- Melt the chocolate and butter together.

- Place a layer of aubergines in the bottom of the prepared tin. Spread over some of the chocolate mixture and then some Morello conserve. Continue layering, ending with a chocolate layer. Leave in a cool place, but not in the fridge, until the chocolate has set.

- To serve, sprinkle with sifted icing sugar.

PANFORTE DI SIENA

A speciality from Siena, this flat cake has a nougat-like texture, and is rich in candied peel, toasted nuts and spices. It has become a traditional Christmas speciality.

SERVES 8-10

75g (3oz) hazelnuts
75g (3oz) blanched almonds
175g (6oz) candied peel
25g (1oz) cocoa powder
50g (2oz) plain white or Italian type '00' flour
2.5ml (½ teaspoon) ground cinnamon
1.25ml (¼ teaspoon) ground mixed spice
100g (4oz) sugar
100g (4oz) honey
For the topping
30ml (2 tablespoons) icing sugar
5ml (1 teaspoon) ground cinnamon

- Pre-heat the oven to 150°C, 300°F, Gas Mark 2. Line a 20cm (8 inch) flan ring with parchment paper.

- Spread the hazelnuts and almonds on a sheet of foil, under the grill, and toast until golden, turning them frequently. Roughly chop the hazelnuts and almonds and finely chop the candied peel.

- Put the nuts, candied peel, cocoa powder, flour, cinnamon and mixed spice in a bowl and mix well together.

- Put the sugar and honey in a saucepan and heat gently until a sugar thermometer registers 115°C, 240°F or until a little of the mixture, dropped into a cup of water, forms a ball. Immediately remove from the heat, add to the nut mixture and, working quickly, mix well.

- Turn into the prepared tin and, using a tablespoon dipped in hot water, spread the mixture flat, making sure that it is no more than 1cm (½ inch) thick.

- Bake in the oven for 30 minutes. Leave to cool in the tin, then turn out onto a wire rack and peel off the paper. Sprinkle the top thickly with sifted icing sugar and cinnamon and serve cut into small wedges.

MY GRANDMOTHER ITALIAN GATEAU

Torta della Mia Nonna

I have the most wonderful memories of this cake being served at special family gatherings, birthdays and feast days. It can also be used as an Italian wedding cake. Do make it for your own family celebrations.

SERVES 10-12

For the cake
6 free range eggs
175g (6oz) caster sugar
175g (6oz) plain white or Italian type '00' flour

For the confectioners' custard
30ml (2 tablespoons) plain white Italian type '00' flour or cornflour
30ml (2 tablespoons) caster sugar
1 free range egg
grated zest of 1 unwaxed lemon
2.5ml (½ teaspoon) vanilla extract
300ml (½ pint) milk

For the butter cream
175g (6oz) unsalted butter

175g (6oz) plus 15ml (1 tablespoon) icing sugar
1 free range egg
100ml (3½fl oz) cold, strong, black coffee

For the topping
45ml (3 tablespoons) rum
300ml (½ pint) double cream
a few drops vanilla extract
75ml (5 tablespoons) toasted flaked almonds or hazelnuts, or a mixture of both
seasonal fruit such as peaches, nectarines, strawberries, to decorate

- Pre-heat the oven to 190°C, 375°F, Gas Mark 5. Grease and line a 30cm (12 inch) or a 23cm (9 inch) deep, round cake tin and dust with flour.

- To make the cake, put the eggs and sugar in a bowl and stand over a saucepan of gently simmering water. Using an electric whisk, whisk until thick and creamy. Gently sift in the flour, a little at a time, and fold in.

- Pour into the prepared tin. Bake the 30cm (12 inch) cake for 18-20 minutes or the 23cm (9 inch) cake for 35-40 minutes until risen and golden. Turn out and cool on a wire rack.

- To make the custard, in a small bowl mix together the flour or cornflour, sugar, egg, lemon zest and vanilla extract. Gently heat the milk in a saucepan, but do not allow to boil. Gradually pour into the egg and flour mixture. Return to the saucepan and heat very gently, stirring constantly with a wooden spoon, until the mixture thickens. Remove from the heat and place a piece of parchment paper over the custard to prevent a skin forming. Leave to cool.

- To make the butter cream, in a bowl beat together the butter and 175g (6oz) icing sugar. In a separate bowl, beat the egg with the 15ml (1 tablespoon) sugar. Add the egg and sugar mixture to the butter mixture. Using an electric whisk, gently add the coffee and mix until thick and creamy.

- To assemble the cake, cut the cake horizontally into 3 even slices. Spoon the custard on one layer and spread the butter cream on the second layer. Sandwich the cake slices together. Gently pour over the rum to soak into the cake.

- Whip the cream and vanilla extract until it just holds its shape, then use to cover the top and sides of the cake. Carefully press the nuts on to the sides and decorate the top with the prepared fresh fruit. Chill before serving.

APRICOT ALMON
SHORTCAKE

Tortino ricaperto di Albicocche

This is the best shortcake recipe I know. It is delicious and really melts in the mouth. It's a great treat for all the family on a special day.

SERVES 8-10

For the shortcake
125g (4oz) unsalted butter
125g (4oz) caster sugar
1 free range egg
100g (3½oz) self-raising flour
100g (3½oz) plain white or Italian type '00' flour

For the filling
40g (1½oz) unsalted butter
30ml (2 tablespoons) caster sugar
1 egg yolk
2-3 dashes vanilla extract

25g (1oz) ground almonds
30ml (2 tablespoons) plain white or Italian type '00' flour
225g (8oz) fresh apricots

For the topping
125g (4oz) ground almonds
45ml (3 tablespoons) caster sugar
6 egg yolks and 2 egg whites
15ml (1 tablespoon) Amaretto liqueur
125g (4oz) apricot conserve
50g (1oz) toasted flaked almonds

- Grease and line a deep, 20cm (8 inch) loose-bottomed cake tin.

- To make the shortcake, put the butter and sugar in a large mixing bowl and beat together until light and creamy. Add the egg and beat well. Stir in the self-raising flour and plain flour. Turn out on to a lightly floured surface and knead lightly until smooth. Wrap in greaseproof paper and chill in the fridge for 30 minutes.

- Meanwhile, make the filling. Put the butter, sugar, egg yolk and vanilla extract in a small bowl and beat until light and fluffy. Stir in the almonds and flour. Put the apricots in a food processor or blender and blend until smooth. Gently fold into the almond mixture.

- Pre-heat the oven to 170°C, 325°F, Gas Mark 3.

- Divide the shortcake dough in half. On a lightly floured surface, roll out each half to a 20cm (8 inch) round. Place 1 round into the prepared tin.

- Spread the filling mixture over the shortcake dough, to within 1cm (½ inch) of the edge. Place the second round of dough over the apricot mixture and gently press the edges together, to seal.

- Brush with water, then bake in the oven for 30-35 minutes until pale golden brown. Leave to stand for 15 minutes before turning out on to a wire rack to cool. Remove the paper lining carefully and place on a baking tray.

- To make the topping, put the almonds and sugar in a mixing bowl. In a small bowl, mix together the egg yolks and Amaretti, then gradually stir into the almond mixture. Remove ¼ of the mixture and add 10ml (2 teaspoons) unbeaten egg white. Mix well together and use to spread over the sides of the shortcake.

- Whisk 1 egg white until stiff and fold into the reserved almond mixture. Spoon into a piping bag, fitted with a large, star nozzle. Pipe zigzag lines in a pattern over the top of the shortcake and pipe small rosettes around the edge.

- Bake in the oven at 200°C, 400°F, Gas Mark 6 for 8-10 minutes until the top is lightly browned.

- Meanwhile, heat the apricot conserve until melted, then sieve into a bowl.

- Spoon two-thirds of the apricot conserve between the zigzag lines and leave for 10 minutes to cool. Spread the sides with the remaining apricot conserve and coat with the toasted almonds. Leave to cool before serving.

PALERMO SWEET FIG AND NUT CAKE

Buccellato Palermitano

Sweet fig and nut cake has many regional variations. This particular recipe, from Palermo, will make two small cake rings. They make a great gift for Christmas, wrapped in cellophane and tied with a ribbon.

MAKES 2, EACH TO SERVE 6

For the filling
225g (8oz) figs
75g (3oz) candied orange peel
50g (2oz) hazelnuts
50g (2oz) unblanched almonds
50g (2oz) fresh walnuts
50g (2oz) raisins
1.25ml (¼ teaspoon) ground cloves
60ml (4 tablespoons) apricot conserve

For the dough
450g (1lb) plain white or Italian type '00' flour
5ml (1 teaspoon) baking powder
225g (8oz) unsalted butter
pared rind of 2 lemons
75g (3oz) caster sugar
150ml (¼ pint) milk
4 large free range eggs, lightly beaten
1 large free range egg, beaten, for glazing

- Pre-heat the oven to 190°C, 375°F, Gas Mark 5. Grease baking trays.

- Chop the figs into small pieces and put in a bowl. Finely chop the candied orange peel, chop the hazelnuts, almonds and walnuts, and add to the figs with the raisins. Add the cloves and apricot conserve, mix well together, cover and set aside.

- To make the dough, sift the flour and baking powder into a large bowl. Rub in the butter until the mixture resembles fine breadcrumbs. Finely chop the pared lemon rind and stir into the flour with the sugar. Add the milk and the 4 beaten eggs and mix until a smooth dough is formed.

- Turn the dough onto a well floured surface and lightly knead until smooth. Divide the dough in half. Roll out one half of the dough into a 30cm (12 inch) round.

- Spread half of the filling to within 1cm (½ inch) of the edge. Roll up like a Swiss roll, making sure that the roll sits on its seam. Bring the two ends together to form a ring. Place on the prepared baking tray. Repeat with the remaining piece of dough.

- Brush with the remaining egg and bake in the oven for 50 minutes until golden brown, firm to the touch and crisp and golden on the bottom. Cool on a wire rack.

FRESH GRAPE AND FENNEL FLAT BREAD

Schiacciata di Uvetta e Finocchio

This sweet flat bread is best served warm as an accompaniment to coffee or as a dessert. Schiacciata means squashed, as the grapes are squashed on the top, and it is made to celebrate the grape harvest in October. It can also be made with raisins soaked in Vin Santo inside and fresh grapes on top.

SERVES 4-6

15g (½oz) fresh yeast or 10ml (2 teaspoons) dried yeast
175ml (6fl oz) hand-hot water
50g (2oz) caster sugar plus 30ml (2 tablespoons)
350g (12oz) strong white flour
5ml (1 teaspoon) salt

45ml (3 tablespoons) olive oil
450g (1lb) black grapes, preferably seedless
1.25-2.5ml (¼-½ teaspoon) fennel seeds
beaten egg, for glazing

- Brush a large, edged baking tray with oil.

- Cream the fresh yeast with the water (if using dried yeast, sprinkle if into the water with a pinch of the sugar and leave in a warm place for 15 minutes until frothy).

- Put the flour, salt and 30ml (2 tablespoons) sugar in a large bowl. Make a well in the centre, add the yeast liquid and the oil and beat together to form a soft, slightly sticky dough, adding a little more flour if necessary.

- Turn on to a floured surface and knead lightly until just smooth. Put in an oiled bowl, cover with a clean tea-towel and leave in a warm place for about 1 hour until doubled in size.

- Meanwhile, halve and, if necessary, remove the seeds from the grapes. Put in a small bowl with the 50g (2oz) sugar and the fennel seeds. Cover and leave to marinate while the dough is rising.

- On a well floured surface, roll out half the dough to an oblong measuring about 28x25cm (11x10 inch). Place on the prepared baking tray and top with three-quarters of the grapes, fennel seeds and juices, spreading to within 1cm (½ inch) of the edge of the dough. Cover with the remaining dough, dampening and sealing the edges well.

- Brush with the beaten egg to glaze and spoon over the remaining grape mixture. Leave in a warm place for 15-20 minutes or until doubled in size.

- Pre-heat the oven to 200°C, 400°F, Gas Mark 6.

- Bake in the oven for 35-40 minutes or until well browned. Serve warm, cut into squares.

EASTER DOVE

Colomba di Pasqua

Traditionally enjoyed at Easter, throughout Italy, this special, enriched cake in the shape of a dove has variations from village to village.

MAKES 2, EACH TO SERVE 6

20g (¾oz) fresh yeast or 10ml (2 teaspoons) dried yeast
175ml (6fl oz) hand-hot milk
400g (15oz) plain white or Italian type '00' flour
100g (4oz) unsalted butter
3 large free range eggs and 1 egg yolk
100g (4oz) caster sugar

2.5ml (½ teaspoon) salt
5ml (1 teaspoon) vanilla extract
grated zest of 1 orange
grated zest of 1 unwaxed lemon
65g (2½oz) raisins
65g (2½oz) mixed candied peel
icing sugar, for dusting
100g (4oz) whole, blanched almonds

- Blend the yeast with the warm milk then leave for 15 minutes until frothy.

- Stir in 100g (4oz) of the flour, cover and leave for 30 minutes.

- Melt the butter and leave to cool. Whisk together the eggs, egg yolk and sugar, then whisk in the butter.

- Stir in the salt, vanilla, orange and lemon zests. Add the remaining 300g (11oz) flour and mix together with a wooden spoon.

- Beat in the yeast mixture until the mixture is smooth. Mix in the raisins, reserving 2, and the candied peel. Place the dough in an oiled bowl, cover with a clean tea-towel and leave for 1¾-2 hours until doubled in size.

- Draw the outline of a dove shape on to 2 sheets of parchment paper. Line 2 baking trays with the parchment sheets.

- Turn out the dough on to a lightly floured surface and knead for 2-3 minutes. Divide in half and shape each piece into a dove and place each dove on a separate baking tray. Use the reserved raisins for the eyes.

- Cover with a clean tea-towel and leave to rise again at room temperature for about 1 hour until double the size. Stud the doves with the almonds.

- Pre-heat the oven to 190°C, 375°F, Gas Mark 5.

- Bake the Easter Doves in the oven for about 15-18 minutes until golden brown and firm to the touch. Transfer to a wire rack and leave to cool. Dust with sifted icing sugar before serving.

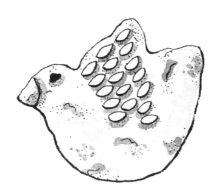

PANETTONE

Panettone comes from Milan in Northern Italy. The cakes are exported in attractive tall boxes, which can be seen hanging in Italian delicatessens all over the world. Panettone made at home is not so tall as the commercial varieties, and its texture is not quite so open, but it makes a deliciously light alternative to heavy Christmas fruit cakes.

SERVES 9 FROM 3 SMALL PANETTONE

350g (12oz) plain white or Italian type '00' flour
20g (¾oz) fresh yeast or 11.25ml (2¼ teaspoons) dried yeast
225 ml (8fl oz) hand-hot milk
100g (4oz) unsalted butter, softened

3 egg yolks
50g (2oz) caster sugar
75g (3oz) chopped candied peel
50g (2oz) sultanas
7.5ml (1½ teaspoons) grated nutmeg

- Grease the insides of three 400g tomato cans, or similar. Cut 3 strips of baking parchment, each measuring 55x30cm (22x12 inch). Fold each piece in half lengthways then use to line the tins. Line the bases with a circle of baking parchment.

- To prepare the dough, sift the flour into a large bowl and make a well in the centre. Blend the fresh yeast with 30ml (2 tablespoons) of the milk until smooth, then stir in the remaining milk. If using dried yeast, sprinkle it into the milk and leave in a warm place for 15 minutes until frothy.

- Add the yeast liquid to the flour and mix well together, gradually drawing in the flour from the sides of the bowl. Knead for 10 minutes until smooth. Form into a ball and place in a lightly oiled bowl. Cover with a clean tea-towel and leave to stand in a warm place for 45 minutes or until doubled in size.

- Add the softened butter to the dough with 2 of the egg yolks, the sugar, candied peel, sultanas and nutmeg. Mix well together. Cover and leave to stand again in a warm place for a further 45 minutes or until doubled in size.

- Divide the dough into 3 pieces and knead each piece for 2-3 minutes. Form each piece into a smooth ball and place inside the cans. Leave in a warm place for about 30 minutes or until risen to the top of the cans.

- Pre-heat the oven to 200°C, 400°F, Gas Mark 6. Brush over the remaining egg yolk. Bake in the oven for 20 minutes, then lower the temperature to 180°C, 350°F, Gas Mark 4 and bake for a further 20 minutes or until a skewer inserted in the centre comes out clean. Leave to cool in the cans.

- The Panettones can be stored in an airtight tin for up to 1 week.

Biscuits and Cookies

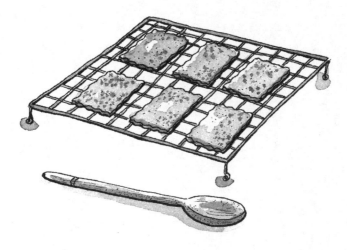

In Italy, biscuits are so important to serve with coffee, with ice cream or to dip into Vin Santo at the end of a meal. There are literally thousands, each village having their own particular favourite recipe. Again, I've chosen my favourites, including Almond Curls, Twice Baked Cookies and some special ones for feast days, such as All Souls' Biscuits. They are all simple to make at home, and children, especially, will always come back for more, particularly for the Almond and Cherry cookies from my village.

ALMOND AND CHERRY COOKIES

Biscotti di Mandorle et Ciliege
(See colour photograph)

These bring back warm childhood memories to me and, with their lovely, crumbly texture, are popular with all children.

MAKES 15

100g (4oz) unsalted butter	150g (6oz) self-raising flour
50g (2oz) caster sugar	15 whole blanched almonds
a few drops of vanilla extract	15 glacé cherries

- Preheat the oven to 180°C, 350°F, Gas Mark 4. Grease several baking trays.

- Melt the butter. Add the sugar, vanilla extract and then the flour and mix to form a firm dough.

- Shape the mixture into 15 balls and top each with an almond and a cherry. Arrange on the baking tray, leaving plenty of room between each, as they will spread. Bake in the oven for 10-15 minutes until golden.

- Transfer to a wire rack and leave to cool.

SPICED CHRISTMAS COOKIES

Biscotti di Natale Aromatici

These delicious cookies can be enjoyed throughout the year and are good served with fresh coffee, Vin Santo or ice cream. I serve these to my newly-arrived students at the cookery school in Umbria. They disappear quickly as they are always popular.

MAKES 28

100g (4oz) Amaretti biscuits (almond macaroons)
25g (1oz) dried figs
65g (2½oz) caster sugar
50g (2oz) plain white or Italian type '00' flour
25g (1oz) ground almonds
dash of vanilla extract
grated zest of ½ an unwaxed lemon

2.5ml (¼ teaspoon) baking powder
2.5ml (¼ teaspoon) ground cinnamon
25g (1oz) sultanas
1 egg white
15ml (4 tablespoons) dry white wine
icing sugar, for sprinkling

- Pre-heat the oven to 180°C, 350°F, Gas Mark 4. Grease several large baking trays.

- Finely grind the Amaretti biscuits and chop the figs. Put in a bowl with all the remaining ingredients except the egg white, wine and icing sugar.

- Make a well in the centre and add the egg white and wine and mix to form a stiff dough. On a lightly floured surface, knead vigorously for about 10 minutes. (The dough will become stickier when kneaded.)

- Shape the dough into flat cookies, the size of chestnuts, and place on the prepared baking trays.

- Bake in the oven for 18-20 minutes until dry and the surface is slightly cracked. Transfer onto a wire rack and leave to cool.

- Sprinkle with sifted icing sugar before serving. Store in an airtight tin.

.

TWICE BAKED COOKIES

Biscotti alle Mandorle

These cookies are called Biscotti *in Italian. They are baked twice, which makes them dry and ideal for dipping into Vin Santo at the end of a meal. There are many variations of these cookies – you may want to experiment using hazelnuts instead of almonds.*

MAKES 24

275g (10oz) plain white or Italian type '00' flour	2 free range eggs and 1 egg yolk
150g (5oz) caster sugar	5ml (1 teaspoon) vanilla extract
5ml (1 teaspoon) baking powder	100g (4oz) whole blanched almonds

- Pre-heat the oven to 180°C, 350°F, Gas Mark 4.

- Put the flour, sugar, baking powder, eggs, egg yolk and vanilla extract into a bowl and mix well together by hand. Add the almonds and knead until mixed together.

- Divide the dough into 6 pieces, then form each piece into a roll and flatten into a flat cigar shape.

- Arrange on a baking tray and bake in the oven for 20 minutes.

- Remove from the oven and cut each biscuit into 4 pieces then return to the oven and bake for a further 10 minutes until golden. Transfer to a wire rack and leave to cool.

ROLLED BISCUITS

Storti

These biscuits are made in the same way as Ginger Snaps and are famous in Venice. They are eaten with fresh cream that has been whipped with a little sugar and an optional drop of liqueur. The cream and biscuits together are known as Panna con Storti. *They are also delicious served with ice cream.*

MAKES 20-24

155g (5½oz) plain white or Italian type '00' flour	pinch of salt
155g (5½oz) caster sugar	75ml (3fl oz) double dream
	75ml (3fl oz) milk

- Pre-heat the oven to 190°C, 375°F, Gas Mark 5. Grease several baking trays.

- Put all the ingredients in a food processor and mix to form a stiff batter.

- Put 4 heaped tablespoons of the mixture on a prepared baking tray, allowing plenty of room for spreading.

- Bake in the oven, in batches, for 10-12 minutes until golden around the edges. Remove from the oven and immediately roll each biscuit around the handle of a wooden spoon. Hold each biscuit until it forms into a roll then transfer to a wire cooling rack and leave to cool.

SWEET PASTRY BEANS

Fave Dolci Romane

Fave *means broad bean in Italian and this is the shape of these biscuits. They are traditionally made for All Saints' Day.*

MAKES 30

15g (½oz) unsalted butter plus extra for greasing
175g (6oz) plain white or Italian type '00' flour plus extra for dusting
100g (4oz) sugar
100g (4oz) whole blanched almonds
5ml (1 teaspoon) ground cinnamon
1 free range egg, beaten
grated zest of 1 lemon
icing sugar, for dusting (optional)

- Pre-heat the oven to 180°C, 350°F, Gas Mark 4. Butter several baking trays and dust with flour.

- Put the sugar and almonds in a food processor and blend until finely ground.

- Put the flour and cinnamon in a bowl and rub in the butter. Add the almonds and sugar, egg and lemon zest and mix together until the mixture is firm and smooth.

- Roll the dough into a thin, long cylinder, then divide into pieces the size of a walnut. Shape each piece to resemble a broad bean.

- Place on the baking trays and bake in the oven for 15 minutes until light golden in colour. Transfer to a wire rack to cool and become crisp. If liked, dust with sifted icing sugar before serving.

ORANGE AND ALMOND COOKIES

Baci di Dama

This recipe is taken from my previous book, Real Fast Vegetarian Food, *and I am including it again here because it has proved so popular with my friends.* Baci di Dama *actually means kiss of the dame, translated literally.*

MAKES 12

100g (4oz) candied orange peel
100g (4oz) ground almonds
100g (4oz) caster sugar
100g (4oz) plain white or Italian
type '00' flour
about 90ml (6 tablespoons) milk
50g (2oz) dark chocolate with 70
per cent cocoa solids

- Pre-heat the oven to 180°C, 350°F, Gas Mark 4. Line several baking trays with parchment paper.

- Very finely chop the orange peel and put in a bowl. Add the almonds and sugar and sift in the flour, reserving 15ml (1 tablespoon). Mix well together, then add enough milk to form a smooth, firm dough.

- Roll the mixture into 24 small balls and place, well apart, on the baking trays. Sprinkle with the remaining flour.

- Bake in the oven for 15 minutes until golden brown. Transfer to a wire rack and leave to cool.

- Melt the chocolate and use a little to sandwich the cookies together in pairs.

COFFEE KISSES

Baci di Caffè

These are light and delectable. I particularly enjoy them after a siesta.
The coffee filling gives you a needed boost.

MAKES 6

2 free range eggs
125g (4oz) caster sugar
125g (4oz) self raising flour
60ml (4 tablespoons) cornflour
For the filling
3 egg yolks
50g (2oz) caster sugar

30ml (2 tablespoons) plain white or
    Italian type '00' flour
225ml (8fl oz) milk
15ml (1 tablespoon) finely ground
    fresh coffee
100ml (4fl oz) double cream
icing sugar, for dusting

- Pre-heat the oven to 180°C, 350°F, Gas Mark 4. Grease several baking trays.

- Put the eggs and sugar in a mixing bowl and beat together until thick and creamy. Sift the flour and cornflour together, then fold through the egg mixture in two batches.

- Spoon 12 heaped tablespoonfuls of the mixture onto the baking trays, allowing plenty of space for spreading. Bake in the oven for 10 minutes until pale golden and firm to the touch. Transfer to a wire rack and leave to cool.

- To make the filling, whisk together the egg yolks, sugar and flour until thick and creamy. Gently heat the milk and coffee in a saucepan but do not allow to boil. Gradually whisk the milk mixture into the egg mixture. Return the mixture to the saucepan and heat, stirring, until the mixture thickens. Remove from the heat, cover with greaseproof paper and leave to cool.

- Whisk the cream until stiff. When the filling is cold, fold in the cream.

- To serve, spread the filling over the flat side of half of the Coffee Kisses and top each with another Coffee Kiss. Dust with icing sugar and serve immediately.

ITALIAN LADY'S FINGERS

Savoiardi

As the name suggests, Savoiardi *come from Savoy, which is north-west of Turin in the Piedmonte region of Italy.* Savoiardi *are used in a range of other desserts. In Italy, they are given to children as a snack. Make up a batch and store in an airtight tin so that they are always available.*

MAKES 12

3 free range eggs, separated	5ml (1 teaspoon) baking powder
5ml (1 teaspoon) vanilla extract	1.25ml (¼ teaspoon) salt
75g (3oz) self-raising flour	75g (3oz) caster sugar

- Pre-heat the oven to 180°C, 350°F, Gas Mark 4.

- Beat the egg yolks until thick, then beat in the vanilla extract. Sift the flour and baking powder together.

- Whisk the egg whites until stiff, then whisk in the salt and sugar until the whites are glossy and very stiff.

- Using a metal spoon, fold in the egg yolks, then the sifted flour.

- Drop tablespoons of the batter onto an ungreased baking tray, forming fingers measuring about 20x6cm (8x2½ inch).

- Bake in the oven for 10 minutes until golden. Transfer to a wire rack and leave to cool.

ALL SOULS' BISCUITS

Ossa dei Morti

These biscuits are brittle and dry like old bones, that's how they got their rather macabre Italian name, meaning Bones of the Dead. They are eaten all over Italy during 1st and 2nd November to celebrate All Souls' Day.

MAKES 18-20

175g (6oz) blanched almonds
175g (6oz) dark chocolate with 70 per cent cocoa solids
2 egg whites
100g (4oz) icing sugar

175g (6oz) semolina flour
For the topping
175g (6oz) dark chocolate with 70 per cent cocoa solids
25g (1oz) unsalted butter

- Pre-heat the oven to 180°C, 350°F, Gas Mark 4. Line several baking trays with baking parchment.

- Roughly chop the almonds and chocolate. Whisk the egg whites until stiff, then gradually add half the sugar until well mixed and the mixture is shiny and stiff. Sprinkle in the remaining sugar. Add the semolina flour, chopped almonds and chocolate and fold in well.

- Using 2 teaspoons, shape small portions of the mixture, on the baking trays, into bone-shaped biscuits about 7.5cm (3 inch) long and 4cm (1½ inch) wide. Space the biscuits well apart to allow for spreading.

- Bake in the oven for 30 minutes until the biscuits are fairly dry but still pale. Transfer to a wire rack and leave to cool in the oven.

- For the topping, melt together the chocolate and butter. Dip the bones into the chocolate and spread over evenly. Place on a wire rack and leave to set before serving.

CHOCOLATE CHERRY BISCUITS

Biscotti Ripieni al Cioccolato con Ciliegia

Italians indulge in these biscuits as a treat after Lent. Of course, you can enjoy them at any time of the year.

MAKES 24

350g (12oz) plain white or Italian type '00' flour
2.5ml (½ teaspoon) baking powder
125g (4oz) unsalted butter, softened
2 large free range eggs, lightly beaten

75g (3oz) sugar
40g (1½oz) blanched almonds
30–45ml (2-3 tablespoons) cherry conserve
125g (4oz) dark chocolate with 70 per cent cocoa solids

- In a large bowl, sift the flour and baking powder. Add the butter and, using your hands, work the butter into the flour until the mixture is coarse. Add the eggs and sugar and mix with your hands until a ball of dough is formed. On a lightly floured surface, knead the dough until smooth. Wrap in greaseproof paper and chill in the fridge for 1 hour.

- Pre-heat the oven to 180°C, 350°F, Gas Mark 4. Lightly grease several baking trays.

- Finely chop the nuts. Put the dough on a floured surface and, using a rolling pin, flatten the dough. Sprinkle the nuts over the surface and knead them into the dough with your hands.

- Divide the dough in half. Roll out one half into a 30cm (12 inch) square. Trim the edges so that they are straight. With a fluted pastry wheel, cut the dough widthways into 8 rows and lengthways into 6 rows. The biscuits should be 4x5cm (1½x2 inch). Repeat with the remaining dough. Place the biscuits well apart on the baking trays.

- Bake in the oven for 10-15 minutes until lightly browned. Transfer to a wire rack and leave to cool.

- When cold, spread the jam on half the biscuits and sandwich them together in pairs.

- Melt the chocolate and, using a small spoon, spread a little of the chocolate evenly over the top of each biscuit. Place on a wire rack and leave to dry completely before serving.

ALMOND CURLS

Biscotti Rotolino

These biscuits are real favourites served with Italian Vanilla Ice cream (see page 103) – or any other ice cream for that matter!

MAKES 18

150g (5oz) ground almonds
75g (3oz) caster sugar
pinch of ground cinnamon

grated zest of ½ an unwaxed lemon
2 egg whites

- Pre-heat the oven to 180°C, 350°F, Gas Mark 4. Grease and line several baking trays with baking parchment.

- Mix together the almonds, sugar, cinnamon and lemon zest.

- Whisk the egg whites until stiff then fold into the almond mixture.

- Put the mixture in a piping bag fitted with a large nozzle and pipe out on to the baking trays in an S-shape, 5cm (2 inch) long. Allow plenty of space for spreading.

- Bake in the oven for 10 minutes until golden . Transfer to a wire rack and leave to cool.

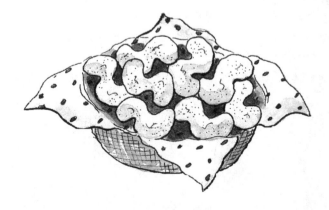

CORNMEAL BISCUITS

Gialletti

These are delicious, crisp Tuscan biscuits. Serve them with coffee for breakfast, as we do in Italy.

MAKES 28

100g (4oz) unsalted butter
200g (7oz) plain white or Italian type '00' flour
300g (11oz) fine polenta
100g (4oz) caster sugar

3 free range eggs, beaten
100ml (3½fl oz) milk
5ml (1 teaspoon) vanilla extract
icing sugar, for dusting (optional)

- Melt the butter. Put the flour, polenta and sugar into a large bowl and pour in the eggs, milk, butter and vanilla extract. Mix well together. Turn out onto a lightly floured surface and knead the dough. Wrap in greaseproof paper and chill in the fridge for 30 minutes.

- Pre-heat the oven to 180°C, 350°F, Gas Mark 4. Grease several baking trays.

- On a lightly floured surface, roll out the dough to 2cm (¾ inch) thick and, using a 6cm (2½ inch) fluted or plain cutter, cut into rounds. Place on the prepared baking trays.

- Bake in the oven for 15 minutes until crisp and yellow. Transfer to a wire rack and leave to cool.

- Store in an airtight jar. If wished, serve dusted with sifted icing sugar.

SARDINIA MACAROONS

Germinus

This recipe was given to me by my friend Antonietta in Umbria, who has a fabulous pastry shop. Be sure to use fresh almonds for the best results.

MAKES 25-30

2 egg whites
175g (6oz) caster sugar

175g (6oz) flaked almonds
5ml (1 teaspoon) lemon juice

- Pre-heat the oven to 170°C, 325°F, Gas Mark 3. Cover several large baking trays with baking parchment.

- Beat the egg whites until stiff. Fold in the sugar, almonds and lemon juice. Place heaped teaspoonfuls of the mixture, well apart, on the baking trays.

- Bake in the oven for about 20 minutes until lightly coloured. Leave to cool. Store in an airtight container.

Gifts of Food

There can be nothing better, in my opinion, than a gift of food. It is a typical Italian habit to visit friends or family with something good to eat or drink as an offering. These gifts are suitable for any occasion throughout the year. Many, such as Chocolate Truffles, can be gift wrapped and given as a present on birthdays, at Christmas and Easter. Do make use of the seasonal harvests to prepare some of my favourite ideas for presents, particularly the Elderflower Champagne.

ELDERFLOWER CHAMPAGNE

Bacca di Sambuco

In Italy, when elderflowers are out, you will see many Italian ladies wandering amongst the hedgerows, picking basketfuls of flowers. Make sure the elderflowers are open and creamy white when you pick them. This is so simple to make and quite delicious.

MAKES ABOUT 4.5 LITRES (8 PINTS)

700g (1½lb) sugar
grated zest and juice of 4 large
   unwaxed lemons

30ml (2 tablespoons) white vinegar
12 elderflower heads

- Put the sugar and 450ml (1 pint) water in a saucepan and heat until the sugar has dissolved. Leave to cool.

- Add the lemon zest and juice to the sugar syrup. Pour into a large bowl and add 4 litres (7 pints) of water and the vinegar. Float the elderflowers, heads down, on the top and leave for 36 hours.

- Strain through muslin and pour into clean, screw-top bottles.

- Store in a cool, dark place for 3 weeks before drinking. Open with caution as it really is champagne.

LEMONCELLO

This liqueur is made throughout the whole of Southern Italy and is given to guests at the end of a meal. It calls for fine lemons so always use unwaxed ones for a great flavour. In Italy, we use pure alcohol to make this liqueur. I do realise that it is difficult to find everywhere so vodka is a good alternative, as it has a neutral flavour.

MAKES 1.2 LITRES (2 PINTS)

6 unwaxed lemons	225g (8oz) sugar
75cl bottle vodka or pure alcohol	450ml (¾ pint) pure bottled water

- Put the lemons in a bowl of cold water and leave to soak for 1 hour. Remove from the water and dry with kitchen paper.

- Using a vegetable peeler, carefully peel the zest from the lemons, taking care no white pith remains.

- Put the lemon zest in a wide-mouthed jar. Pour over the vodka and cover. Leave in a dark place for 20 days.

- After 20 days, put the sugar and 450ml (¾ pint) water in a saucepan and bring to the boil, stirring to dissolve the sugar. Remove from the heat, cover and leave until cold.

- When cold, add the sugar mixture to the lemon zest mixture. Strain the mixture, pour into bottles and seal. Leave in a cold, dark place for 7 days before serving.

- Serve cold and, once opened, store in the fridge.

GREEN WALNUT LIQUEUR

Nocino

My friends in Lama, Umbria introduced me to this luscious liqueur and I have included it for those lucky enough to have a walnut tree. It's quite wonderful served with ice cream.

MAKES ABOUT 2.8 LITRES (5 PINTS)

1.4kg (3lb) fresh green walnuts
2.3 litres (4 pints) vodka or pure
  alcohol
1 clove

1 small cinnamon stick
1.7 litres (3 pints) dry red wine
225g (8 oz) granulated sugar

- Wash and dry the walnuts then put in a large jar and pour in the alcohol. Add the clove and cinnamon. Close the jar tightly and leave for 2 months.

- To make the syrup, put the wine and sugar in a saucepan and heat gently for 1 hour until reduced to a light syrup. Leave to cool.

- When cold, mix the syrup with the contents of the jar, then strain through a colander or sieve. Pour into bottles and seal. Leave the bottles for 10 days before using. Store in a cool, dark place until required.

ORANGE LIQUEUR

Liquore al Mandarino

This recipe comes from southern Italy, where there is an abundance of citrus fruits and using some of them to make this delicious liqueur is an excellent idea.

MAKES ABOUT 2.6 LITRES (4½ PINTS)

3 mandarin or tangerine oranges
1.4 litres (2½ pints) pure alcohol or

unflavoured vodka
350g (12oz) granulated sugar

- Wrap the oranges in muslin and tie with string into a parcel. Pour the alcohol into a jar and suspend the parcel in the alcohol. Cover the jar with a lid and leave for 28 days.

- To make the sugar syrup, put the sugar and 900ml (1½ pints) water in a saucepan and heat gently until the sugar has dissolved. Leave to cool.

- When cold, add the syrup to the alcohol. Pour into bottles, seal and leave for 4 days before using. Store in a cool, dark place until required. Once opened, store in the fridge.

CHERRIES PRESERVED IN RUM

Ciliegie Sotto Spirito

There are many varieties of cherries, the most common being Maraschino and Amoree cherries. These are large, dark and sweet and are grown in the south of Italy. Use the preserved cherries in tarts and cakes, or serve with ice cream.

MAKES ABOUT 1KG (2LB)

1kg (2¼lb) ripe cherries
1 cinnamon stick
thickly pared zest of 1 unwaxed
   lemon

100g (4oz) caster sugar
200ml (7fl oz) rum
pure alcohol or vodka, if necessary

- Wash and dry the cherries and pack them tightly into a jar. Add the cinnamon and lemon zest.

- Dissolve the sugar in the rum and pour onto the cherries. Fill the jar with alcohol or vodka if necessary. Cover and seal.

- Leave in a warm place for 8 weeks, shaking and turning the jar occasionally. Store in a cool, dark place until required.

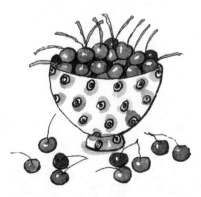

MUSCATEL RAISINS IN WINE

Uva Passa

This makes a great present and my father just loves it. Muscatel raisins are available from health food shops. It is always wonderful served with ice cream.

MAKES ABOUT 450G (1LB)

300g (11oz) Muscatel raisins
thickly pared zest of 3 unwaxed
 lemons
300ml (½ pint) sweet white wine

20ml (4 teaspoons) lemon juice
15ml (1 tablespoon) rum
 (optional)

- Fill a jar with the raisins, add the lemon zest and cover with the wine, lemon juice and rum if using. Cover and seal.

- Leave for at least 1 week before using, to allow the fruit to absorb the alcohol. Store in a cool, dark place for up to 1 year.

FIGS IN VIN SANTO

Fichi in Vin Santo

Vin Santo is a strong, white, dessert wine from Tuscany. The lemon cuts into the sweetness of the wine and figs and balances the flavour – I cannot think of a better marriage. Serve with ice cream or mascarpone cheese.

SERVES 4-6

22 dried figs
250ml (8fl oz) Vin Santo or sweet dessert wine

30ml (2 tablespoons) lemon juice
grated zest of 2 unwaxed lemons

- Cut the tough tops off the figs. Put in a saucepan with the Vin Santo and heat to simmering point, then poach for about 15 minutes until tender. Add the lemon juice and zest and stir well together. Leave to cool.

- When cold, drain the figs, reserving the liquid. Pack the figs into jars and cover with the syrup. Cover and store in a cool, dry, dark place for up to 18 months.

APRICOTS IN SWEET WHITE WINE

Albicocche in Vino Bianco Dolce

Apricots remind me of two things: the approach of summer and my mother – she just adores them. I particularly like them when they have a blush on their skin, which is a sign that they are ripe and at their best.

MAKES ABOUT 550G (1¼LB)

700g (1½lb) fresh apricots	15ml (1 tablespoon) lemon juice
150g (5oz) sugar	75cl bottle of sweet white wine

- Wash and halve the apricots, discarding the stones. Pack the apricots as tightly as possible into bottling jars and cover with the remaining ingredients, leaving a 2.5cm (1 inch) space at the top. Cover the jars, turning the screw-bands back a quarter-turn.

- Place the jars in a large, deep saucepan, immersed up to their necks in cold water. Bring the pan to the boil and simmer for 1½ hours. Make sure the water temperature reaches 82°C (180°F) during the 1½ hours and maintain it there for 10 minutes.

- Remove the jars from the pan one at a time, place on a wooden surface and immediately tighten the screw-bands. Leave to cool. Store in a cool, dark place for up to 1 year.

QUINCE JELLY

Cotognata

I first enjoyed this quince jelly on a trip to Sicily with my father. It is traditional to eat it at the end of a meal. Every family has its own special recipe and this one has been handed down from generation to generation, along with the pottery moulds.

MAKES ABOUT 900G (2LB)

olive oil, for brushing
900g (2lb) quinces

900g (2lb) sugar
juice of 1 unwaxed lemon

- Brush the insides of some small, shallow moulds or pots with oil.

- Peel, core and quarter the quinces. Put in a heavy-based saucepan with just enough water to cover the bottom of the pan and simmer gently for about 30 minutes until soft. Remove from the heat.

- Turn into a food processor or blender and add the sugar and lemon juice. Blend until smooth.

- Return to the heat and simmer, stirring constantly, until the sugar is completely dissolved and the mixture is very thick and comes away from the sides of the pan.

- Pour into the prepared moulds to a depth of no more than 2.5cm (1 inch). Leave to set and cover as for jam.

- Store in a cool dry place for up to 1 year. Turn out to serve.

CANDIED ORANGE OR LEMON ZEST

Arancia Candita e Limone Candito

This is a speciality from southern Italy. So many oranges and lemons are grown there and this is one way of using their precious skins. Consequently, candied zest appears in many southern Italian recipes.

275g (10oz) granulated sugar
2 smooth-skinned oranges or

lemons
caster sugar, for sprinkling

- To make the syrup, put the sugar and 600ml (1 pint) water in a saucepan and heat until dissolved. Boil for 90 seconds.

- Wash and dry the oranges or lemons. Using a swivel-blade vegetable peeler, peel the zest off the fruit, then slice the zest into matchsticks or other shapes you might want.

- Add the zest to the syrup and boil for 5 minutes if matchsticks, 10 minutes if larger. Using a slotted spoon, lift them out of the syrup and cool on wire racks.

- Sprinkle with caster sugar and roll the zest in the sugar until well coated. Shake off any excess sugar and store the zest in an airtight box.

ALMOND STUFFED FIGS IN CHOCOLATE

Fichi Secchi con Mandorle e Cioccolato

This is a delicacy from the Calabria region of Italy. Figs are plentiful in Italy and this is a wonderful way of using them. They are so good to make for a gift – perhaps even more so where figs are less common.

MAKES 12

12 whole blanched almonds
pared zest of 3 oranges
12 dried figs, preferably Italian

225g (8oz) dark chocolate with 70 per cent cocoa solids

- Spread the almonds on a sheet of foil under the grill, and toast until golden, turning them frequently. Finely chop the orange zest.

- Slit the figs and place an almond inside each. Roll the figs in the orange zest.

- Break the chocolate into a heatproof bowl standing over a saucepan of simmering water and heat until melted. Using a fork, dip the figs in the chocolate, then place on baking parchment and leave to dry.

SESAME NOUGAT

Torrone di Sesamo

This particular recipe demonstrates the extensive use of honey and almonds in Italian cooking. Sesame seeds are full of calcium, and almonds are good for you, too, so don't feel guilty about enjoying this recipe.

MAKES ABOUT 48 SQUARES

200g (7oz) fragrant honey
50g (2oz) caster sugar
225g (8oz) sesame seeds
200g (7oz) blanched, toasted
almonds, roughly chopped
30ml (2 tablespoons) almond or
sunflower oil

- Brush a baking tray and rolling pin generously with oil.

- Put the honey in a saucepan and heat gently until melted. Add the sugar and slowly bring to the boil.

- Add the sesame seeds and almonds and heat, stirring all the time, until the mixture thickens.

- Pour onto the baking tray and flatten with the rolling pin into a square measuring about 28cm (11 inch) and 5mm (¼ inch) thick. Leave to cool slightly.

- Using a sharp knife, cut into squares measuring about 4cm (1½ inch). Leave to cool completely. Store in an airtight tin.

CHOCOLATE TRUFFLES

Tartufi al Cioccolato
(See colour photograph)

These are the most scrumptious, wickedly rich truffles, and they really do make the perfect gift at any time of the year. Wrap them in clear cellophane, or indulge in a small gift box for them and you have a present anyone will welcome.

MAKES 12

50g (2oz) petit beurre biscuits	30g (1¼oz) raisins
25g (1oz) hazelnuts	1 tablespoon rum
75g (3oz) dark chocolate with 70 per cent cocoa solids	cocoa powder, for dusting

- Put the biscuits in a polythene bag and crush with a rolling pin. Finely chop the hazelnuts.

- Melt the chocolate and mix with the biscuits. Add the remaining ingredients, except the cocoa powder, and mix together. Leave to cool for 1 hour.

- Form the mixture into small balls the size of a cherry and dust with cocoa powder. Place in little sweet papers and store in a cool, dry place.

CHOCOLATE SALAMI

Salame al Cioccolato

This is a rather special chocolate and biscuit mixture in the shape of a salami. It is easy to make and goes beautifully with coffee at the end of a meal. Take it as a gift when you go to eat with friends and everyone will enjoy it.

SERVES 6-8

50g (2oz) split blanched almonds
20 petit beurre biscuits
225g (8oz) dark chocolate with 70 per cent cocoa solids
175g (6oz) unsalted butter

45ml (3 tablespoons) brandy
25g (1oz) ground almonds
15ml (1 tablespoon) cocoa powder for dusting

• Spread the blanched almonds evenly in a grill pan and grill for 2-3 minutes, shaking the pan frequently, until golden.

• Put the nuts in a food processor and finely grind. Transfer to a bowl.

• Put the biscuits in the food processor and blend until roughly crushed. Set aside 15ml (1 tablespoon) and put the rest in a bowl.

• Break the chocolate into pieces and put in a small saucepan. Cut the butter into small pieces, add to the chocolate with the brandy and heat gently until melted.

• Pour the melted chocolate mixture into the bowl of crushed biscuits, add the nuts and mix well together. Leave in the fridge for about 2 hours until the mixture is solid.

• Sprinkle the reserved biscuit crumbs onto a piece of baking parchment and turn the chocolate mixture onto it. With a palette knife and your hands, shape into a sausage about 23cm (9 inch) long and roll in the biscuit crumbs.

• Wrap in the baking parchment and leave in the fridge for about 3 hours until the mixture is solid. Unwrap, slice into rounds to serve and dust with cocoa powder.

The Cook's Own Pages

Use these pages to note your favourite recipes, any adaptions you've made to them and to keep a record of the recipes you have served when entertaining.

Index

If you enjoyed
Italian Cakes and Desserts,
why not try Ursula Ferrigno's bestselling
Real Fast Vegetarian Food?

Just cut out this order form and pass it on!

ORDER FORM

REAL FAST VEGETARIAN FOOD
by Ursula Ferrigno

'I love her food – it makes life worth living.' –
Malcolm Gluck

Anybody can create delicious, colourful and inspirational food with the minimum of fuss with Ursula Ferrigno's *Real Fast Vegetarian Food*. Recipes range from *Wild Mushroom and Basil Tart* to *The Richest Chocolate Cake Ever*. Illustrated with beautiful line drawings throughout, this guide to modern vegetarian cooking is the perfect reference book or present.

Ursula Ferrigno is a passionate vegetarian cook and former principal tutor for Cordon Vert. Half-Italian by birth, she brings a Mediterranean theme to her recipes and her food is stocked by companies ranging from Harvey Nichols to Concorde.

224 pages; Demy format; 30 black and white line illustrations

---

TO ORDER: ring your local bookshop or our Freefone credit card hotline on 0500 418 419.